Rescued by

Word for Windows

Allen L. Wyatt

JAMSA
P·R·E·S·S
...a computer user's best friend

a division of Kris Jamsa Software, Inc.

Published by
Jamsa Press
2821 High Sail Ct.
Las Vegas, NV 89117
U.S.A.

For information about the translation or distribution of any Jamsa Press book, please write to Jamsa Press at the address listed above.

Rescued by Word for Windows

Printed in the United States of America.
98765432

ISBN 0-9635851-4-2

Publisher	*Technical Editor*
Debbie Jamsa	Kevin Hutchinson
Copy Editor	*Illustrator*
Paul Medoff	Phil Schmauder
Composition	*Indexer*
Kevin Hutchinson	Ken Cope
Cover Design	*Cover Photograph*
Jeff Wolfley & Associates	O'Gara/Bissell
Layout Design	
Discovery Computing	

Table of Contents

Section One

LEARNING THE ROPES

Word for Windows is a powerful software program that can help you make your words look the best they can. Before you can start using Word for Windows effectively, though, you must learn the basics—the skills that act as a foundation for everything you do in the program. This section will provide you with the information you need to build a firm foundation. Here you will learn how to start and stop the program, how to get help, and how to change what you see on your screen. You will learn about the tools used in Word for Windows and how to get around in your document. By the time you finish this section, you will have mastered many of the skills necessary to grow and develop effectively with Word for Windows.

Lesson 1 *Starting and Ending Word for Windows*

Lesson 2 *Getting Help When You Need It*

Lesson 3 *Positioning Word for Windows*

Lesson 4 *The Word for Windows Environment*

Lesson 5 *How to Get Around Your Document*

Lesson 6 *Selecting Your View*

Lesson 7 *Changing What You See*

Lesson 1

Starting and Ending Word for Windows

If you have been using Windows for any time, there is a good chance you will feel right at home with Word for Windows. The program makes full use of all the features of Windows, including menus, buttons, and bars. In this lesson you will learn the following:

- How to start Word for Windows

- How to use Word for Windows menus

- How menus and options are selected

- How to exit Word for Windows

STARTING WORD FOR WINDOWS

To start Word for Windows, you must first be running the Windows Program Manager, the desktop program that always runs when Windows is running. The Program Manager is where you will most likely start all of your Windows programs; it should look similar to Figure 1.1:

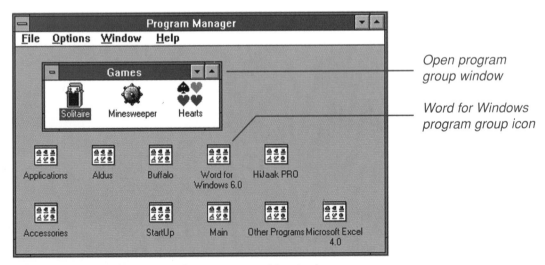

Figure 1.1 Program Manager, showing open and iconized program groups.

Notice that the title bar, at the top of the window, says **Program Manager.** This window contains both icons, which represent *program groups,* and open windows, which are nothing more than program groups that have been opened. One of the program groups or windows on your screen should be titled **Word for Windows.** (This title may, optionally, be followed by a version number, such as **Word for Windows 6.0.**) If this program group is an icon, *double-click* on the icon with the mouse. Double-click means to press the left mouse button twice, in quick succession. When you do this properly, the program group icon should be expanded to an open window, as shown in Figure 1.2:

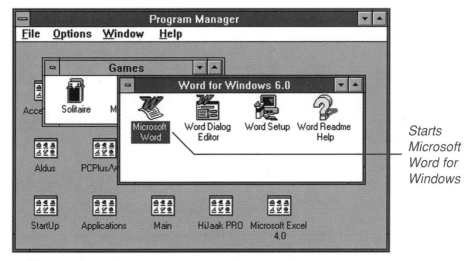

Figure 1.2 Word for Windows 6.0 program group window opened.

Notice that the program group window contains four icons—Microsoft Word, Word Dialog Editor, Word Readme Help, and Word Setup. To start Word for Windows, simply double-click on the Microsoft Word icon; the program will start, and you will see the Microsoft Word program window, as shown in Figure 1.3:

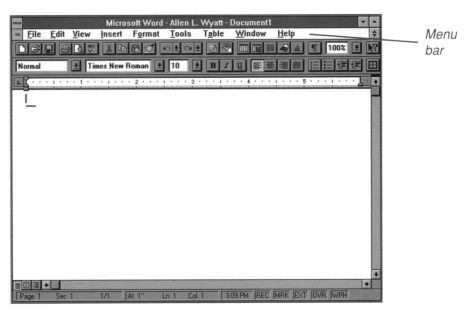

Figure 1.3 *When you start Word, a new document is usually opened.*

When you start Word for Windows, you might actually see a dialog box showing a "Tip of the Day." If you do, this is part of Word for Windows' way of improving your program skills by providing information you might not be aware of. Simply click on OK, and you will see the Microsoft Word program window.

Your screen might differ a little, depending on the options you have set. Over the course of this book you will learn how to use and set the options that control how your screen looks. One thing that should be the same, regardless of the actual appearance of your screen, is the menu bar at the top of the Microsoft Word window. At its simplest, Word for Windows is a word processing program that allows you to work with *documents*. These are nothing more than files that contain text, graphics, and other objects. You will learn about some of these graphics and objects later in this book.

When you start Word for Windows, it typically starts with a brand new document already loaded. If this happens, your menu bar will look like this:

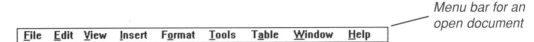

and Word for Windows is ready for you to begin typing. If your menu appears shorter, like this:

*Menu bar when no
document is open*

File   Help

you will need to either create a new document or open an existing one (Lesson 11). To create a document, you will need to use the menu.

USING WORD FOR WINDOWS MENUS

There are two ways you can use a menu. The first is to point the mouse pointer to the menu you want to use and then click on the left mouse button. The other method is to use the keyboard. To do this, you hold down the ALT key and press the underlined letter in the menu name. For instance, to use the File menu, you would press ALT–F.

Whether you use the mouse or the keyboard, selecting a menu results in the menu being displayed. Since you might want to create a new document, you will need to access the File menu (click once on the menu's name). When you do, the menu will *drop down*, as shown in Figure 1.4:

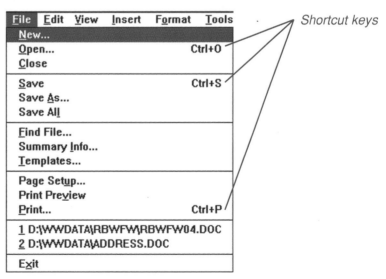

Shortcut keys

Figure 1.4 File menu, dropped down.

Notice that, in the case of the File menu, there are many choices you can make. Not every menu has lots of different choices—some have only a few. The option names are always on the left side of the menu, and a *shortcut key* (if there is one) is displayed at the right side. These shortcut keys indicate ways you can access the option without using the menu. If you wanted to use the keyboard, you could also press the option letter that is underlined.

Word for Windows is a very powerful program that allows you to change just about everything to customize the program to the way you work. This includes the ability to change the menus. If your program has not been customized extensively, there are nine menus that you can use to control the program and affect your document. These are

- **File** Allows you to perform file-related activities, including opening, saving, and printing

- **Edit** Allows you to edit, search, replace, and link text

- **View** Allows you to define options concerning how you want Word for Windows to appear for you

- **Insert** Allows you to insert various types of elements into your document

- **Format** Allows you to define how you want your text or other document element to appear

- **Tools** Provides various tools, which can be used to refine your document. These tools are covered in Section 5, "Using Some Tools"

- **Table** Allows creating, inserting, editing, and deleting tables. Tables are covered in more detail in Section 7, "Working with Tables"

- **Window** Allows you to choose how you view the various document windows, if you have multiple documents open at once (see Section 8, "Word for Windows Shortcuts,")

- **Help** Allows you to get either general or specific help

As you are beginning to work with Word for Windows, there is no better way to get used to the program than to start working with the menus. Go ahead—select various menus and menu options. It won't hurt a thing, and you will begin to see some of what Word for Windows can do for you.

ENDING WORD FOR WINDOWS

When you have finished using Word for Windows, you can exit the program quickly and easily. Remember when you viewed the File menu earlier in this lesson? One of the options from that menu was Exit. This option allows you to exit the program and return to the Program Manager. You can also, however, double-click on the Control menu icon, which is located in the upper-left corner of the window:

If you prefer using the keyboard, pressing ALT–F4 also allows you to leave the program. When you leave, Word for Windows might display the dialog box shown in Figure 1.5:

Figure 1.5 *Select Yes to save document before exiting Word for Windows.*

This simply means that you have made some changes to the document in memory, and Word for Windows wants to find out if you want them saved to disk before you leave the program. Once you leave the program, you cannot recover any information that was not saved. If you want to learn more about saving information in a file, refer to Lesson 10, "Saving Your Document."

WHAT YOU NEED TO KNOW

In this lesson you have had your first encounter with Word for Windows. Since this is the first lesson, important concepts have been covered. You should know how to do the following:

☑ Start Word for Windows

☑ Pull down a menu

☑ Exit Word for Windows

If you are still unclear on any of these items, you will want to read through the lesson again before moving on. Starting, ending Word for Windows, and using the menus are integral to everything else you do in the program.

In the next lesson you will learn how to get Word for Windows help when you need it.

Lesson 2

Getting Help When You Need It

In Lesson 1 you learned how you can start and end Word for Windows. Once you are working with Word for Windows, however, there may be times when you need a little help. This is particularly true if you are just starting out with Word for Windows or if you are using a command that you don't use that often.

Word for Windows provides a great Help system. This help system works basically the same as the Help system in any other Windows program. In this lesson you will learn the following:

- How to access the Help system

- What the parts of the help window are and how they work

- How to access related help topics through the use of interactive links

- How to see definitions of key terms

- How to move through the Help system

- How to search for a Help topic

- How to get context-sensitive help

- How to keep the Help window displayed

ACCESSING HELP

In Lesson 1 you learned about the menu system in Word for Windows. Take another look at the menu bar:

Notice that at the very right side of the menu bar is a choice labeled Help. If you choose this menu, you will see a list of different types of help you can receive, as shown in Figure 2.1.

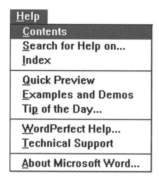

Figure 2.1 *The Help menu.*

There are nine choices from this menu. You can select several of these choices to explore the capabilities of Word for Windows at any time you desire. Several of the choices deserve in-depth explanation, however, since you will probably use them again and again.

The eighth choice, Technical Support, is used when you need to call Microsoft because you have a problem that you cannot resolve in any other way. For instance, if your program simply refuses to act as it should, or if you are interested in receiving an update. The last help choice, About Microsoft Word, will also be used if you call Microsoft. When you choose this item, you will see a dialog box similar to the one shown in Figure 2.2.

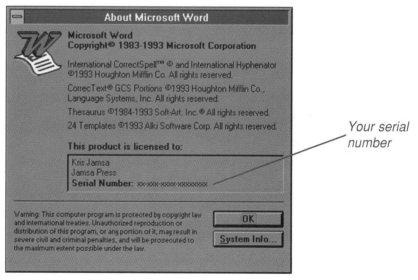

Figure 2.2 *The About Microsoft Word dialog box.*

This provides information about your copy of Word for Windows. It even includes your serial number, which will be needed any time you talk to a technical support person at Microsoft. When you are through viewing the About dialog box, click on [OK].

Select the Index option from the Help menu. When you do, you will see the Help window appear, as shown in Figure 2.3.

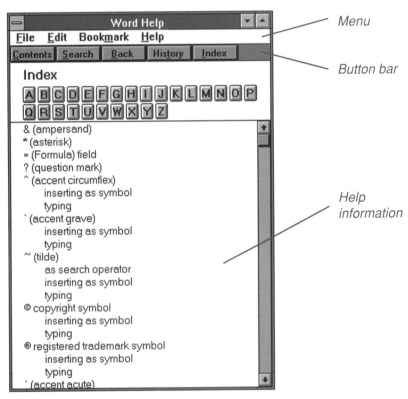

Menu

Button bar

Help information

Figure 2.3 A typical Help window.

The actual appearance of your Help window may be different. For instance, it may be wider, or shorter, or it may be very small. This is because, as you adjust the size of the Help window (as well as its position), it is remembered from one help session to another. So the size and position of the window you currently see is the same as when the Help window was last displayed.

There are three parts to the Help window. The first is the menu, which offers four choices. What these choices do is not necessarily important to getting help about a topic. They are provided for those people who want to load different help files or make changes to the help file currently being used.

The second part of the Help window is the button bar. It appears directly beneath the menu. There are five (and sometimes more) buttons on this bar; most of these will be explained during the course of this lesson.

Finally, there is the body of the Help window. This is where you can see information about a topic. It is in this area where you will get the most information about the subject. You can scroll through this window as you would any other window (see Lesson 5).

When you are through using the Help system, you can close the Help window by double-clicking on the Control menu icon (▬) in the upper-left corner of the Help window. You can also choose the Exit option from the File menu of the Help window.

HELP IS INTERACTIVE

The Help files used by Word for Windows are completely interactive. This means you can quickly access different parts of a Help file. For instance, take a look at Figure 2.4, which shows the help screen that is displayed when you select Contents from the Help menu.

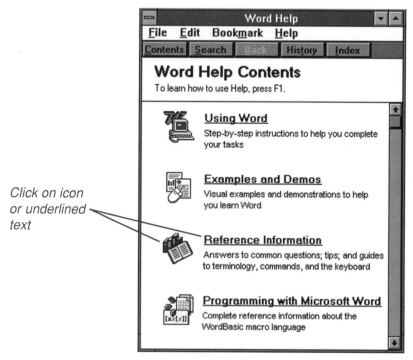

Click on icon or underlined text

Figure 2.4 The Help system Contents screen.

Notice that there are icons on the left side of the dialog box and several terms that have a solid underline. As you move the mouse pointer over these items, it changes to a pointing hand:

Pointing hand cursor

If you click on either the icons or the underlined text when the pointer looks like this, you will be able to receive help related to that item. For instance, if you click on Reference Information icon (or underlined text), you will see the information shown in Figure 2.5.

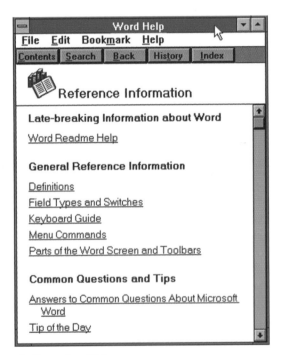

Figure 2.5 *The Reference Information Help screen.*

To get back to the previous screen, use the [Back] button on the button bar. This allows you to step back one screen. If you want to step back more than one screen, you could click on the [History] button. When you do, you will see a dialog box that contains a list of all the help topics you have viewed, as shown in Figure 2.6.

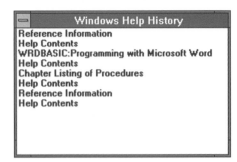

Figure 2.6 *The Windows Help History dialog box.*

You can select any of the listed topics by double-clicking on the topic. If you decide you want to jump back to the contents for the current Help file, all you need to do is click on the Contents button.

There is another feature of the Help system that you should be aware of—the glossary terms. The people who developed Word for Windows understand that there might be terminology used that is new or unusual to you. If you see a term that is underlined with a dashed line, you can view a definition of that term. For instance, the Help screen shown in Figure 2.7 shows both interactive links (solid underlined terms) and glossary terms (dashed underlined terms).

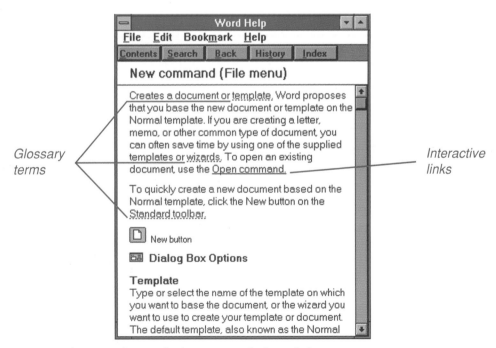

Figure 2.7 *A Help screen showing both interactive links and glossary terms.*

SEARCHING FOR A TOPIC

While you can select a general help topic from the Contents screen, it is often more productive to jump directly to the topic you want to view. This is done by clicking on the [Search] button. When you do, you will see the Search dialog box, shown in Figure 2.8.

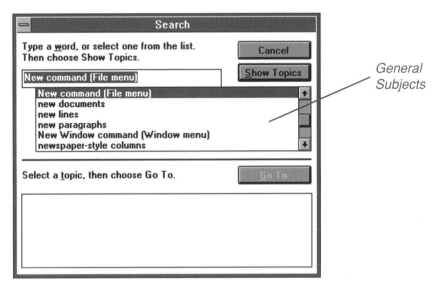

General
Subjects

Figure 2.8 The Search dialog box.

This is divided into two sections. In the top section is a list of general subject areas. You can either scroll through the list with the mouse, or you can start to type a word that begins a topic. As you type, the subject window displays the first subject that closely matches what you are typing. When you have selected a subject, you can click on the [Show Topics] button, and you will see a list of topics for that subject area. These are displayed in the box at the bottom of the Search dialog box, as shown in Figure 2.9.

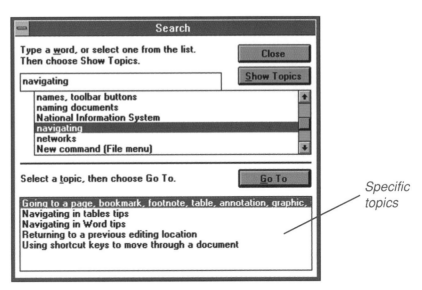

Specific
topics

Figure 2.9 *The Search dialog box with topics displayed.*

Select one of the topics you want to view. If you double-click on the topic, you will see the help information on that topic right away. If you would rather, you can simply select the topic and then click on the Go To button.

HELP ON A MENU TOPIC

Word for Windows allows you to access the Help system by pressing the **F1** key at any time. When you do, Word for Windows will attempt to display help that is appropriate to the task you are performing. This is referred to as *context-sensitive* help, meaning that help is displayed based on the context in which you request the help.

For instance, if you need help concerning Searching (see Lesson 13), then all you need to do is highlight the Find option from the Edit menu, and press **F1.** The Help system is displayed, with the appropriate help information, as shown in Figure 2.10.

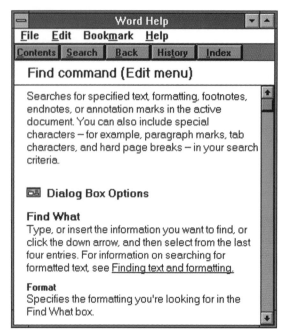

Figure 2.10 The Help screen for the Find command.

This technique will work for any menu item and during the middle of many other operations you might perform in Word for Windows.

KEEPING HELP DISPLAYED

The Help system is simply another Windows program. When you are using help, you normally cannot work on your Word for Windows document at the same time. If you do, the Help window will disappear behind the window used by Word for Windows. However, the Help system has a feature that allows you to keep the Help window displayed at all times. If you select the Always on Top option from the Help menu (of the Help window), you can work on your document while the Help window is displayed. This is great for when you are following a series of steps that might be displayed in the Help window.

WHAT YOU NEED TO KNOW

Word for Windows provides a full-featured Help system that can answer many questions you have about how the program works. After working through this lesson, you should have a pretty good grip on how to use the Help system. In particular, you should know the following:

- ☑ How to access the Help system
- ☑ What the parts of the help window are and how they work
- ☑ How to use interactive links to access related Help topics
- ☑ How to see definitions of key terms
- ☑ How to move through the Help system using the buttons on the Help window button bar
- ☑ How to search for a topic
- ☑ How to get context-sensitive help
- ☑ How to keep the Help window displayed

As you are working with Word for Windows, you will find yourself accessing the Help system often. As you learn different parts of the program, you might have to use it less and less, but there will still be times you will need help for commands and procedures that you do not use daily.

Lesson 3

Positioning Word for Windows

Word for Windows implements the *user interface* of Windows very effectively. A user interface defines how a program appears and interacts with you, the user. You have undoubtedly noticed that this user interface centers on using windows to display information. For the most part, you have control over where and how those windows are displayed. In this lesson you will learn the following information related to Word for Windows:

- The different types of windows used in Windows

- How to control the size of a window

- How adjust the position of window borders

- How to move a window

UNDERSTANDING DIFFERENT WINDOWS

Windows (not just Word for Windows) uses two different types of windows. *Program windows* are used by programs; *document windows* are used to display information within program windows. Generally, document windows are used to contain data used by the program you are running. These two types of windows can typically be told apart by the presence of a menu bar. Program windows, the vast majority of times, have menu bars, and document windows do not.

In Word for Windows, there is only one program window (it contains the menu bar for the Word for Windows program), but there can be multiple document windows. In Lesson 41 you will learn how you can work with more than one document window at a time. I bring this up now so you can understand the relationship between the different windows with which you will be working.

CONTROLLING THE WINDOW SIZE

Whether you are using a document window or a program window, they are both controlled in the same manner. You can adjust the size of both types of windows using the same techniques.

There are three types of sizes for any window. The first is *minimized.* In this condition, a window is reduced to the size of an icon. These are the same type of icons you see when you are working with the Program Manager. The second is *maximized*. In this condition, a window occupies all of the available screen space. If you are working exclusively with one program, you will probably want to maximize the program window for that program. This provides the largest amount of work space. The third window condition is somewhere in between, called *restored*. In this condition you can see other windows on your screen besides the one in which you are working.

So how do you control the size of a window? The easiest method is to use the sizing buttons in the upper-right corner of a window. The three types of buttons you can see are described in Table 3.1:

Button	Function
▲	Clicking on this maximize button will maximize the window; it becomes as large as possible, covering your entire screen.
▼	Clicking on this minimize button will minimize the window, reducing it to the size of an icon. This does not end the program, it simply puts the program aside so you can work on other tasks. Your documents are still available within the program. To open the window again, simply double-click on the icon.
▴▾	This is referred to as the *restore button.* It appears only when a window is maximized, and is used to return a window to its "in-between size."

Table 3.1 Window sizing buttons.

Note: Not all windows can be minimized. Program windows can; however it is up to the program whether document windows can be minimized.

Take another look at the windows in your Word for Windows environment. The sizing buttons may appear like this:

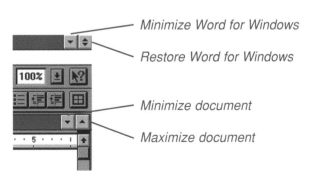

The lower maximize button is associated with your Word for Windows document; it is part of the document window. If you click on this button, the document window is enlarged, and the sizing buttons become this:

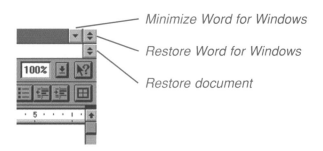

Minimize Word for Windows

Restore Word for Windows

Restore document

The top two sizing buttons control the program window, while the lower one still controls the size of the document window. If you click on the restore button for the document window (that's the lower button), the document window is restored to its smaller size.

Go ahead and restore the size of the document window. Notice that the window no longer fills up the entire program window used by Word for Windows. This prepares you for the next technique you should learn—changing the overall size of a window.

You already know how to make a window as small as possible (minimizing) and how to make one as large as possible (maximizing), but you can also adjust the overall size of the window. This is done by moving the window *borders*, the thin lines surrounding each window. Take a look at the borders of your windows. They should be fairly thin, and they will probably be a different color than other parts of your screen. For instance, in the following corner of a document window, the border is green:

Window border

As you move the mouse cursor so it is positioned over the border, notice that it changes from a single-headed arrow to a double-headed arrow, like this:

Vertical sizing cursor

This is what it looks like when you move the mouse cursor to either of the side borders. The double arrows indicate the directions in which you can move the border. If your cursor is on the top or bottom border, the arrows point up and down. On the side border, the arrows point left and right. If you move the cursor to a corner, they point diagonally, like this:

Horizontal and
vertical sizing cursor

This indicates you can affect two borders at one time—one horizontal and one vertical. When the mouse cursor changes to any of these double arrows, you can move the borders. All you need to do is hold down the left mouse button and move the mouse. As you do, the border moves with the mouse cursor. This is called *dragging* the border. When you are pleased with the positioning of the border, simply release the mouse button. The border will stay where you released the button.

CONTROLLING THE WINDOW POSITION

Moving a window is even easier than changing window size. To move a window, use the mouse pointer to point to the window's title bar. Then click and hold on the left mouse button. As you move the mouse, the window border will move. When you release the mouse button, the window is redrawn at the place where you released the button. Figure 3.1 shows the mouse pointing into the title bar of a document window:

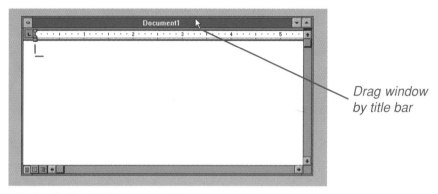

Figure 3.1 *Drag a window by its title bar to move it.*

You can move windows and resize them as you please.

WHAT YOU NEED TO KNOW

One of the benefits of working in the Windows environment is that you can determine how your screen looks. You can rearrange and resize windows as you desire, resulting in a workspace that reflects how you need to work. As you finish this lesson, you should have learned the following information:

- ☑ Windows uses different types of windows; both document and program windows. Each has a different purpose, but can be controlled in the same manner.

- ☑ The minimize button (⬛) allows you to reduce an open window to the size of an icon.

- ☑ The maximize button (⬛) allows you to expand a window so it fills the entire screen.

- ☑ The restore button (⬛) allows you to reduce the size of a window to an "in-between" size.

- ☑ You can change the size of windows by dragging individual window borders to a new position.

- ☑ You can reposition a window by clicking on the title bar and dragging the window to a new position.

Lesson 4

The Word for Windows Environment

As you have already learned, Word for Windows provides a rich environment that allows you to tailor the program to how you work, instead of the other way around. In earlier lessons you performed some of this tailoring. For instance, you learned how to adjust window sizes. As you work throughout this book you will always be learning new ways to change what Word for Windows does. Before you can do that, however, you must learn more about the actual Word for Windows environment. In this lesson you will learn about various parts of the environment, including:

- How to use menus

- What the toolbars are and how they are used

- What the ruler can be used for

- Information provided on the status bar

Take a look at your Word for Windows program window, as shown in Figure 4.1:

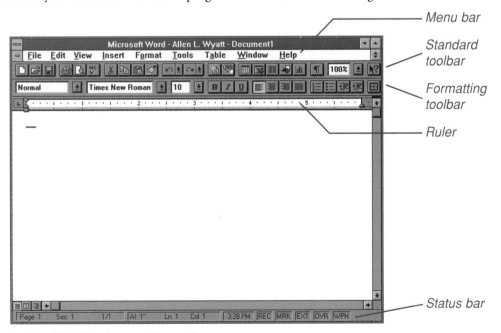

Figure 4.1 Word for Windows, with new document open.

Notice that there are four elements across the top of the screen and one at the bottom. Not all of these elements might be visible on your screen, however. The elements that can be displayed (which are shown in Figure 4.1) are, from top to bottom:

- the menu bar

- the standard toolbar

- the formatting toolbar

- the ruler

- the status bar

The first four items are located at the top of the screen; the status bar is located at the bottom. The menu bar is always visible and cannot be turned off. You learned about how to use the menu bar in Lesson 1. In this lesson you will learn about each of the other elements in the Word for Windows environment.

UNDERSTANDING TOOLBARS

In Word for Windows, a *toolbar* contains a series of buttons as tools. Word for Windows supports multiple toolbars for a variety of purposes. For instance, there are two toolbars displayed here:

One of these toolbars is used for standard functions, and the other is used for formatting. If you cannot see any toolbars on your screen, this is because they are turned off. If you want to display a toolbar, choose Toolbars from the View menu. When you do, you will see the Toolbars dialog box, shown in Figure 4.2:

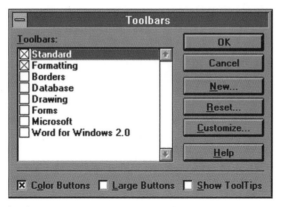

Figure 4.2 *Toolbars dialog box.*

Word for Windows has eight predefined toolbars from which you can choose. You can display any or all of the toolbars. Notice that two toolbars are selected here—Standard and Formatting (as indicated by the checked boxes to the left of the toolbar names). These are the two toolbars shown earlier.

Different toolbars will be used throughout this book for different purposes. Whenever a different toolbar is required, this will be indicated. For most purposes, however, the Standard and Formatting toolbars will do the trick. To follow along with the examples in this book, you should have at least these two toolbars turned on.

THE STANDARD TOOLBAR

The Standard toolbar appears directly beneath the Word for Windows menu, and looks like this:

Normally, there are 22 tools (buttons) on the Standard toolbar. You might actually have more or fewer tools than this, however, based on the toolbars selected and the way they have been customized Assuming that the Standard toolbar is displayed, and it has not been changed by anyone, let's take a look at Table 4.1 to see what each tool represents.

Button	Function
	Creates a new document
	Allows you to load a file—same as choosing Open from the File menu
	Saves the current document to disk—same as choosing Save from the File menu
	Prints a single copy of your document
	Shows how your document will look when printed — same as choosing Print Preview from the File menu
	Checks the spelling in your document—same as choosing Spelling from the Tools menu
	Cuts the selected text, retaining them in the Clipboard—same as choosing Cut from the Edit menu.
	Copies the selected text to the Clipboard—same as choosing Copy from the Edit menu
	Pastes the contents of the Clipboard at the cursor location—same as choosing Paste from the Edit menu
	Copies formatting from one place to another.
	Allows you to undo any of your last X actions
	Allows you to redo any of your last X undone actions
	Automatically formats your document
	Creates or inserts AutoText—same as choosing AutoText from the Edit menu
	Creates a table—same as choosing Insert Table from the Table menu
	Inserts an Excel worksheet in your document.
	Allows you to choose the number of columns in your document—similar to choosing Columns from the Format menu
	Inserts a drawing—displays the Drawing toolbar and allows you to create a drawing, which is inserted at the cursor location
	Inserts a chart—starts Microsoft Graph and allows you to create a chart, which is inserted at the cursor location

Table 4.1 Tools on the Standard toolbar. (continued on next page)

Button	Function
¶	Displays all the nonprinting characters in a document
100% ↴	Current page magnification—click on the value or the arrow to its right to change the magnification
▶?	Inquiry tool—allows you to point to an item on the screen and receive help about it or display information about it

Table 4.1 Tools on the Standard toolbar. (continued from previous page)

As you work with the toolbars, you will come to appreciate the way they can save you time and effort. The tools are always handy, always available on the screen. You will not learn in-depth information about individual tools in this lesson, however. Instead, you will learn about them throughout this book.

THE FORMATTING TOOLBAR

The Formatting toolbar is primarily used for formatting your text. It appears directly beneath the Standard toolbar and looks like this:

You should make sure that the Formatting toolbar is turned on for the examples used in this book.

The Formatting toolbar has both buttons and selection lists. Each of these both indicate the formatting applied to text and change that formatting. Table 4.2 explains each of the sections of the unmodified Formatting toolbar:

Button	Function
Normal ↴	Indicates the style that has been applied to the paragraph. (Styles are discussed in more detail in Section 4.)
Arial ↴	Shows which font has been applied to the selected characters, along with the size of that font. See Lesson 17 for more information on fonts.

Table 4.2 The tools on the Formatting toolbar. (continued on next page)

Button	Function
B *I* **U**	Indicates whether the selected text is bold, italic, or underlined. Any or all of these buttons can be selected to change how characters look. If the selected text includes the attribute, the appropriate button looks like it has been depressed (**B**).
	Change the alignment of a paragraph. The buttons align your text left, center, right, and filled. *Fill-justification* means that the text is aligned with both the left and right margins.
	Creates a numbered list from the selected paragraphs.
	Creates a bulleted list from the selected paragraphs.
	Moves the left margin of the selected paragraphs to the left.
	Moves the left margin of the selected paragraphs to the right.
	Displays the Borders toolbar.

Table 4.2 The tools on the Formatting toolbar. (continued from previous page)

Formatting is a rather extensive topic in Word for Windows because the program allows you to perform many different types of formatting functions. Sections 3 and 4 of this book provide you with complete information about formatting your documents.

THE RULER

The *ruler* is used to indicate margins, tabs, and indents. It appears directly beneath the formatting toolbar, and looks similar to this:

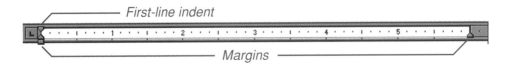

As with the toolbars and the ribbon, the ruler might not be displayed on your screen. In this case, you can use the Ruler option from the View menu to display it. Again, this is a *toggle* option—selecting it again will turn the ruler off. You should turn the ruler on for the examples in this book.

The ruler is divided into units of measurement. The ruler displayed here is divided into inches; your ruler might be divided into different units, such as centimeters, points, or picas. Points and picas are measurement units used in typography and printing. There are approximately 72 points or 6 picas in an inch.

Notice that there is a symbol that appears to the left side of the ruler. This symbol is used to indicate the type of tabs which you can set using the ruler. To change tab types, click on the symbol. Tabs are covered in detail in Lesson 16. There are four different types of tabs available, as shown in Table 4.3:

Icon	Meaning
L	Left-aligned tab
⊥	Center-aligned tab
⌐	Right-aligned tab
⊥	Decimal-aligned tab

Table 4.3 The four tabs in Word for Windows

THE STATUS BAR

At the bottom of the Word for Windows program window is the *status bar*. The status bar displays information about where the cursor is located and the setting of certain toggle keys, provides quick help, prompts you for some types of input, and displays other general status information. The status bar typically looks like this:

If you do not see the status bar on your screen, that is probably because it has been turned off. If you want to check this, select Options from the Tools menu. When you do, you will see a dialog box similar to Figure 4.3:

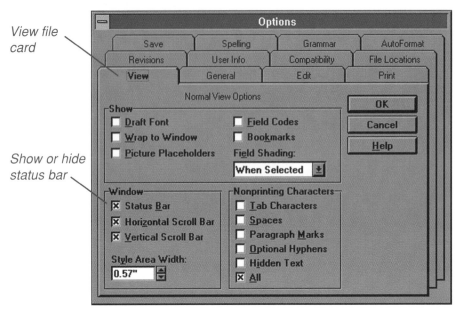

View file card

Show or hide status bar

Figure 4.3 Options dialog box.

This dialog box is used extensively in customizing Word for Windows. In fact, you will use it many times in the course of this book. Notice that the dialog box contains a series of 12 "file cards." The tabs at the top of each file card indicate the category of options on the file card. When you click on one of the tabs, the displayed options change. You should make sure that the View file card is selected (this is the file card displayed in the previous dialog box illustration). If an appears to the left of the Status Bar option on this file card, the status bar should appear at the bottom of the Word for Windows program window. If the does not appear, click on the Status Bar option until it does. When you are satisfied with the setting, click on the [OK] button.

Take a look at the status bar again. The left side of the status bar indicates the current page number, the current section number (see Lesson 9), and how many total page numbers are in the document. The next section of the status bar indicates the current cursor position. The first measurement (At 1") indicates how far the cursor is from the top of the physical page. In other words, where the current line is located relative to the top of a page. The second number (Ln 1) indicates how many lines of text there have been since the top of the page. Thus, in this example the cursor is located on the first line of text on this page. The final number in this section (Col 20) indicates how many characters (including spaces) are to the left of the cursor.

To the right of the position information is the current time, based on the time set in your computer.

WHAT YOU NEED TO KNOW

Word for Windows provides a complete environment in which you can create and format your documents. In this lesson you have learned about several important facets of that environment. In particular, you have learned about:

- ☑ The menus
- ☑ The toolbars
- ☑ The ruler
- ☑ The status bar

A firm understanding of these elements will make your use of Word for Windows much easier and more productive. Before proceeding with the other lessons in this book, make sure you have turned on each of these elements so they are displayed. To turn on display of the toolbars, and ruler, select the appropriate toggle option from the View menu. A check mark next to the option means it is enabled or turned on. To turn on the status bar, select Options from the Tools menu, and then make sure the Status Bar option is selected within the View category. If you have any questions about these procedures, refer to the detailed instructions earlier in this lesson.

Lesson 5

How to Get Around Your Document

It is fairly safe to say that almost all of the documents you create with Word for Windows will be longer than what you can view on one screen. In most instances, your documents will be longer than one page. It is not unusual to have documents extending over many, many pages. In this lesson you will learn how to move through your Word for Windows documents. In particular, you will learn the following:

- How to use the keyboard to move through a document

- How to use the mouse to scroll through a document

- How to jump to specific locations in your document

USING THE KEYBOARD

Using the keyboard to move around your document is very intuitive. If you have used the cursor control keys in other programs, you will probably feel right at home with the use of the keys in Word for Windows. For instance, you can press PGUP or PGDN to move up or down a screen in your document. Likewise, the arrow keys (left, right, up, and down) move the cursor one space in the direction indicated by the arrow.

Some movement is performed by using the cursor control keys in conjunction with other keys. For instance, pressing CTRL-HOME results in moving the cursor to the beginning of the document. Table 5.1 describes the movement actions you can perform with the keyboard.

Key	Alone	With CTRL Key
HOME	Start of line	Start of document
PGUP	Up one screen	Beginning of screen
PGDN	Down one screen	End of screen
END	End of line	End of document
LEFT ARROW	Left one character	Left one word
RIGHT ARROW	Right one character	Right one word
UP ARROW	Up one line	Start of paragraph
DOWN ARROW	Down one line	Start of next paragraph

Table 5.1 Cursor-movement keystrokes.

Don't be put off by the size of this list. Instead, focus on the few keystrokes you will use to do most of your movement. Other keys can be learned as needed.

USING THE MOUSE

To use the mouse to move the cursor, simply point to the position in the document where you want the cursor and click on the left mouse button. Obviously, this can only work if the location where you want the cursor is visible on the screen. If it is not visible, you will need to *scroll* (think of a rolled-up scroll of paper) through your document until the desired text is visible. Scrolling is accomplished by using the *scroll bars* on the screen, shown in Figure 5.1:

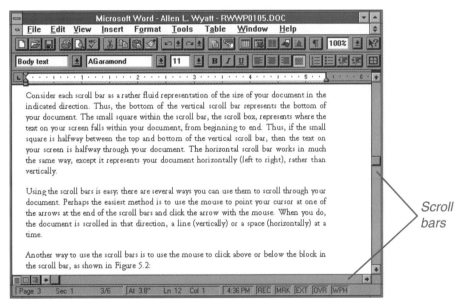

Scroll bars

Figure 5.1 Use scroll bars to view parts of the document that are off screen.

Consider each scroll bar as a rather fluid representation of the size of your document in the indicated direction. Thus, the bottom of the vertical scroll bar represents the bottom of your document. The small square within the scroll bar, the scroll box, represents where the text on your screen falls within your document, from beginning to end. Thus, if the small square is halfway between the top and bottom of the vertical scroll bar, then the text on your screen is halfway through your document. The horizontal scroll bar works in much the same way, except it represents your document horizontally (left to right), rather than vertically.

Using the scroll bars is easy; there are several ways you can use them to scroll through your document. Perhaps the easiest method is to use the mouse to point your cursor at one of the arrows at the end of the scroll bars and click the arrow with the mouse. When you do, the document is scrolled in that direction, a line (vertically) or a space (horizontally) at a time.

Another way to use the scroll bars is to use the mouse to click above or below the block in the scroll bar, as shown in Figure 5.2:

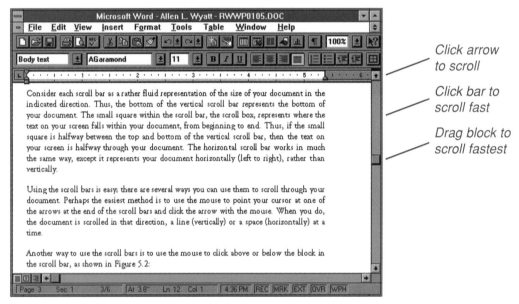

Click arrow to scroll

Click bar to scroll fast

Drag block to scroll fastest

Figure 5.2 Scrolling features in Word for Windows.

When you do, the document is scrolled one screen at a time in the indicated direction.

Finally, you can move large distances by using the mouse to drag the scroll block within the scroll bar. For instance, if you wanted to scroll to the middle of your document, simply point to the block, click and hold down the left mouse button, and then move the mouse. As you do, the block moves as well. When you release the mouse button, the document window is adjusted to display the text at the relative position indicated by the block.

Note: *When you use the scroll bars to move through your document, the cursor does not actually move. Instead, you are only changing what you view on your screen. If you want to move the cursor, you must still point somewhere on your screen and click with the mouse.*

USING THE GO TO FEATURE

If you are working with a large document, you might find using the keyboard or the scroll bars tedious. Instead, can use the Go To feature of Word for Windows. This is accessed in one of two ways—you can either select Go To from the Edit menu or press the **F5** key. When you do, you will see the Go To dialog box shown in Figure 5.3:

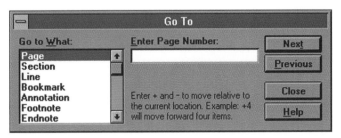

Figure 5.3 *The Go To dialog box.*

Enter a page number and press ENTER. Word for Windows automatically moves the cursor to the beginning of the desired page.

WHAT YOU NEED TO KNOW

Before you can effectively begin working with Word for Windows, you must know how to move around your document. The commands and features presented in this lesson allow you to both move the cursor and scroll the document in many different ways. You have learned how to

- ☑ Use the cursor-control keys to move the cursor
- ☑ Use the mouse and the scroll bars to scroll through the document
- ☑ Use the Go To command to jump to any page in your document.

If you are a bit hazy about how to do any of these tasks, take a minute to review the lesson and find the necessary steps.

Lesson 6

Selecting Your View

When you are using Word for Windows, there are many different viewing modes you can use with your document. The purpose of this lesson is to introduce each of these modes and provide guidelines you can use in determining which view is right for you. By the end of this lesson you will have learned how to:

- Select different viewing modes

- Determine the differences between viewing modes

- Choose the viewing mode that is right for you

- Use zoom magnification to enlarge or reduce your document

The different viewing modes available with Word for Windows can all be accessed from the View menu, as shown in Figure 6.1.

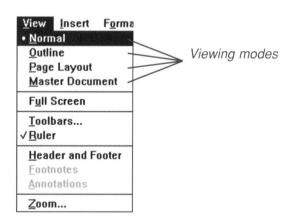

Figure 6.1 *View menu, pulled down.*

The four top menu options are the *viewing modes*: Normal, Outline, Page Layout, and Master Document. The viewing mode currently being used has a small dot (a bullet) to the left of the option. In this example, Word for Windows is using Normal viewing mode. Let's take a look at each viewing mode in a little more detail.

NORMAL VIEWING MODE

Normal viewing mode is how most people will use Word for Windows. In this mode, the screen shows a fairly good approximation of how your final text will appear. When you change fonts (as covered in Lesson 17), you will see the changes reflected in the text on the screen, which will also change appearance. The number of characters per line and the spacing between lines also reflect what will be printed on the final page.

In Normal viewing mode, graphics also appear in text as they will when printed. In other words, you will be able to see the picture on the screen, at the position in the document where it was placed.

This viewing mode was not designed to display pages in their final layout. For instance, you will not be able to see headers and footers (see Lesson 19) on your screen as they will appear in the final printout. Columns (Lesson 14) are not shown in their final position (multiple columns won't be placed next to one another), and page breaks simply appear as lines across the page, as shown in Figure 6.2:

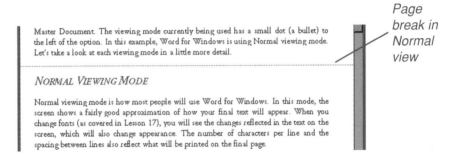

Page break in Normal view

Figure 6.2 Page break in normal view.

To select Normal viewing mode, choose Normal from the View menu.

OUTLINE VIEWING MODE

Outline viewing mode is used for "the big picture." This simply means that you can view and manipulate your document based on headings. Later in this book you will learn how you can format text using styles (see Section 4). If you format text using a specific head level (a style), you can use Outline mode to view just those heads. Alternatively, you can view or hide the text under each head. When you later delete or move the heads, all the text under those heads is deleted or moved as well.

For the most part, outlining is beyond the scope of this book. If you want to use outlining, you should refer to either the online Help system (see Lesson 2) or to your Word for Windows documentation.

PAGE LAYOUT VIEWING MODE

This viewing mode is a step above (toward more completely representing the page as it will be printed) Normal viewing mode, but a step below Print Preview (described in Lesson 12). When you use Page Layout viewing mode, your document is displayed very close to how it will look when it is printed. You can see how the text and other document elements will be placed on the paper, and you can see a pictorial representation of the edge of the paper. This is because you see an actual representation of the sheet of paper. Elements that don't print in Normal viewing mode show up on the page—items such as page headers and footers. Graphics and multiple columns also appear in their proper places in the document.

Because of the amount of processing which must be done to display information in Page Layout mode, you should not use it unless you have to or unless you have a fast computer. If you have a slower computer (one based on the 80286 or on an older 80386), Word for Windows will be unacceptably slow in Page Layout mode.

To select Page Layout viewing mode, choose Page Layout from the View menu.

MASTER DOCUMENT VIEWING MODE

This final viewing mode is brand new with Word for Windows 6.0. It is similar in nature to the Outline viewing mode, in that it allows you to get a look at the "big picture" of your document. However, it is different, in that the parts of the entire document come from smaller subdocuments. A master document, then, is nothing but a "collection point" for the subdocuments. By dividing a project into master and subdocuments, it is conceptually easier to work with and divide among individuals working on the project.

As with outlining, master documents and subdocuments are beyond the scope of this book. If you want to use this Word for Windows feature, you should refer to either the online Help system or to your Word for Windows documentation.

FASTER VIEWING

To display information even faster on your screen, you can use two other settings within Word for Windows. These options are accessed by selecting Options from the Tools menu and making sure that the View file card is selected. The Options dialog box on your screen will look similar to Figure 6.3:

View
file card

Use to speed
up display

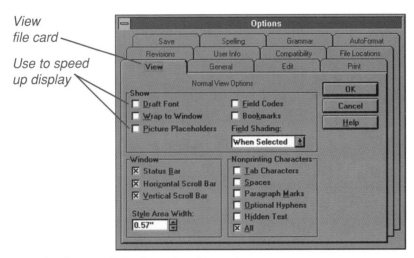

Figure 6.3 Options dialog box, view file card.

The options you are interested in are labeled Draft Font and Picture Placeholders. If you are using Page Layout viewing mode, both of these options will not be visible. That is because Draft Font is only applicable with the other Word for Windows viewing modes. To understand how Draft Font and Picture Placeholders affect your display, take a look at the following part of a document window, displayed in Normal viewing mode in Figure 6.4:

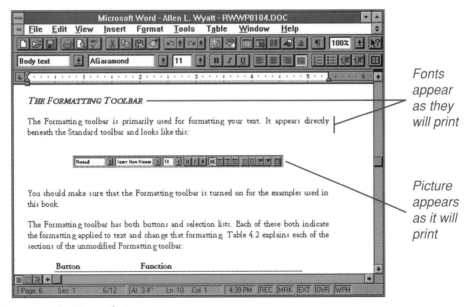

Fonts
appear
as they
will print

Picture
appears
as it will
print

Figure 6.4 Document in Normal view.

Figure 6.5 shows the same document displayed with Draft Fonts and Picture Placeholders selected:

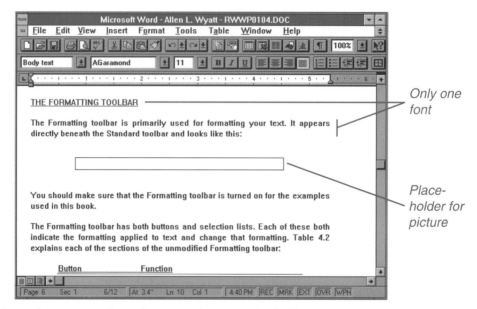

Figure 6.5 Same document, with Draft Fonts and Picture Placeholders selected.

Notice that the text is displayed in a single font, and graphics are not displayed. In this way, Word for Windows can display information quicker than it would otherwise. This is because the program does not have to go through all the math functions necessary to display the normal font and graphics information.

Selecting a Viewing Mode

The viewing mode you use will depend primarily on personal preference and the type of performance you want from Word for Windows. As a general rule, the closer the display is to what the final printed output will be, the slower the program will work. To make your decision about which viewing mode you want to use for your work, you might want to begin with Page Layout mode. If the program is too slow for your tastes, then step down to Normal viewing mode. If the program is still too slow, adjust the View settings.

QUICK REVIEW

The four major viewing modes available in Word for Windows are

- Normal
- Outline
- Page Layout
- Master Document

In addition, you can use Draft Fonts and Picture Placeholders to affect how Normal, Outline, and Master Document viewing modes are displayed. For most of your everyday work, you will probably work in Normal viewing mode, using the other viewing modes only sparingly.

ZOOMING

You will remember from Lesson 5 that the Standard toolbar, at the top of the Word for Windows program window, contains a value that indicates the size at which you are viewing the current screen:

Zoom factor

This number is often called a *zoom factor*. A zoom factor of 100% indicates you are viewing the document at full size. You can adjust the zoom factor by using either the zooming tool on the Standard toolbar or by using the Zoom option from the View menu. When you choose this option, you will see the Zoom dialog box similar to the one shown in Figure 6.6:

Predefined zoom factors

Custom zoom factor

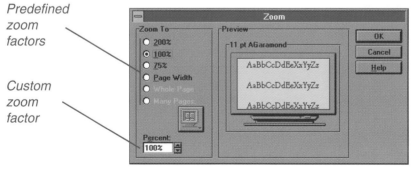

Figure 6.6 Zoom dialog box.

There are six predefined zoom factors available from this dialog box. Three of these zoom factors are expressed as percentages (200%, 100%, and 75%). The other three predefined zoom factors are Page Width, Whole Page, and Many Pages. These adjust your display based on your screen resolution and the available space within your screen. You can also create a custom zoom factor by entering any percentage between 10 and 200 in the Percent box.

Note: Adjusting the zoom factor does not affect your printout. It only changes the size at which you view your document. In fact for most uses, you might never change the zoom factor. It is typically changed when you are working with very small type or with detailed graphics.

WHAT YOU NEED TO KNOW

Word for Windows provides many different ways you can view your document. In this lesson you have learned the following:

- ☑ How to choose Normal, Outline, Page Layout, or Master Document views
- ☑ How to turn on Draft mode
- ☑ How to select the viewing mode that is right for you
- ☑ How to use the Zoom function within Word for Windows

In the next lesson you will learn more about how you can customize what Word for Windows shows you about your document.

Lesson 7

Changing What You See

In Lesson 6 you learned how Word for Windows lets you change what you view. In this lesson you will see how you can change which types of characters you see on your screen. In particular, you will learn how to display or hide any of the following

- Tabs
- Spaces
- Paragraph marks
- Optional hyphens
- Hidden text

If you think about it for a moment, you are probably already aware that there are nonprinting characters that Word for Windows does not normally display. For instance, when you press the SPACEBAR, you can see the effect of your action (the cursor moves one space to the right), but you cannot see the character itself. Instead, all you see is a bit of a space. Another example is when you press the ENTER key. You see the action (the cursor moves to the next line, at the left side of the screen), but you don't see the actual character.

While this may not seem much of a problem to the casual Word for Windows user, it can be critical to those who use the program often. For instance, take a look at the following two lines:

Spaces   Between
Spaces   Between

Which of the two lines has only one space between the words? If you answered the bottom line, you are wrong. Surprised? It is because the bottom line has two spaces in between, and the top has five. There is no good rule of thumb for judging these distances, either. The actual amount of space allotted to a space character varies, depending on the font, the point size, and the line justification. (Don't worry if these terms are unfamiliar to you; they will be introduced fully in later lessons.)

To overcome this confusion and potential problem, Word for Windows allows you to control which characters are displayed on your screen. This is done by choosing Options from the Tools menu. When you do, you will see the Options dialog box. It will probably look like Figure 7.1:

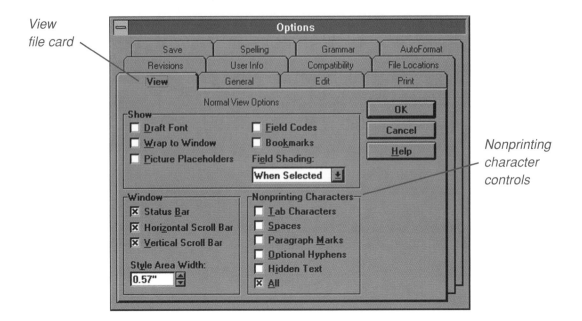

Figure 7.1 *The Options dialog box.*

This dialog box consists of 12 file cards that each control different categories of options within Word for Windows. To change the category being viewed, click on the labeled tab at the top of each file card. Notice that the View category is selected in this illustration. If this same category is not selected on your screen, click on the View tab.

Parts of this dialog box should already look familiar to you. For instance, you learned about the status bar in Lesson 4, about the scroll bars in Lesson 5, and the viewing options in Lesson 6. For this lesson, you should pay particular attention to the right side of the dialog box—to the box titled **Nonprinting Characters**. This box has check boxes in it for each of the following items:

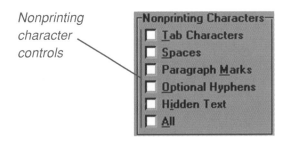

To display a particular special character, select the check box next to it. If the check box is unselected, the corresponding special character will not be displayed on the screen. The character is still there—it is simply not displayed. The other important item to remember is whether or not you display these special characters, they will not print in your final document.

Let's take a look at each of the special characters you can have Word for Windows display.

TAB CHARACTERS

Tabs are inserted when you press the TAB key. Typically this is done if you want to align information horizontally in your document. The trouble is, if you can't see where you have pressed the Tab key, you don't know for sure if you pressed TAB or the SPACEBAR to align the information—they both appear the same.

When you select this option, tabs appear as right-pointing arrows. For instance, the following text is separated by tabs:

Tab characters

Parts → 12.34
Labor → 56.78
Total → 69.12

SPACES

Earlier in this lesson you learned how easy it is to lose track of how many spaces you have inserted in your text. If you select this option, Word for Windows will display a small dot wherever a space is in your text. For instance, the following is the same text presented earlier in the lesson, but this time with the spaces displayed:

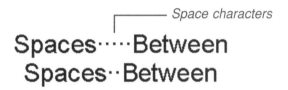

Space characters

Spaces·····Between
Spaces··Between

Now it is easy to determine that there are five spaces on the first line and two on the second. Some people, however, may find these dots distracting. Some may also feel that they are too easily confused with periods. If you turn them on, however, you will quickly discover that you can adjust. The benefits provided by knowing where your spaces are far outweigh any short-term confusion you might experience.

PARAGRAPH MARKS

You may already have noticed that when you press ENTER, Word for Windows advances the cursor to the next line at the left side of the screen. Later in this book, however, you will learn that it is possible for you to define (with styles) how far the cursor should advance when you press ENTER. For instance, you might want to leave a blank line between the current paragraph and the following. Word for Windows makes this quick and easy.

This formatting power, however, is an easy source of confusion for those who are used to pressing ENTER a second time to insert the extra blank line. When they try to "back up" by pressing the BACKSPACE key, it doesn't appear that Word for Windows is doing what they expect because that "extra" blank line is deleted by just pressing the BACKSPACE key once. This confusion can be easily removed, however, by turning on the display of paragraph marks. When you click on this check box, your text appears as follows:

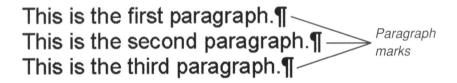

The paragraph symbol is familiar to those who have worked with words in the past. Traditionally, it signifies that a new paragraph is to start at that point. Word for Windows is no exception—that is exactly what is signified here.

OPTIONAL HYPHENS

As you will learn in later lessons, Word for Windows allows you to hyphenate words in your document automatically. These hyphens are considered *optional hyphens*, meaning they only appear if the word is eligible to be hyphenated. If you hyphenate the document and then insert text in the paragraph that pushes the word to the next line, the hyphen disappears. It is still in the text, but does not show up.

If you instruct Word for Windows to display optional hyphens, these hyphens will always be visible. You can tell them apart from regular dashes (which are considered hyphens) by a downward-pointing "hook" that appears on the right side of the hyphen.

If you primarily work with documents that are not hyphenated, then setting this display option provides no benefit.

HIDDEN TEXT

Hidden text is, effectively, text whose display and/or printing you can turn on or off. In Word for Windows, it is a text attribute you can turn on or off, the same as bold or italics. You will learn more about how to use hidden text later in this book.

Normally, hidden text is not displayed. It is saved with the document, but it does not show up on your screen. To view hidden text, turn on this option. This text then appears with a thin, dashed underline, as shown here:

Hidden text underline

This is hidden text.
This is normal text.

ALL

If you click on this option, it doesn't really matter which other characters you have chosen to display. Word for Windows displays all optional nonprinting characters. Why (you might ask) is there such a setting in Word for Windows? Couldn't you simply make sure all the other check boxes are selected?

Well, you could. But the primary reason for including the All option is not to save you from the necessity of clicking the other check boxes. Instead, this is meant as a temporary "show everything" setting. The setting of this check box is the same as clicking the ¶ button on the Formatting toolbar—all the nonprinting characters are displayed.

The real advantage of this setup is that you can choose, from the individual check boxes, just those nonprinting characters you normally want to see. For instance, you might only care to display paragraph marks and tabs. Fine—click on those, and that is all you will see. But if you later want to see all the characters, choose the ¶ button. When you have finished and want to return to your default setting (paragraph marks and tabs), click on ¶ again. Now your document is displayed exactly as you are used to it.

WHAT YOU NEED TO KNOW

Every character you type in a document is maintained and tracked by Word for Windows. This includes characters that don't normally print or are not normally visible on your screen. Using some of the customization features of Word for Windows, you can control exactly what you see on your screen. After finishing this lesson, you should know how to control whether Word for Windows displays each of the following:

- ☑ Tabs
- ☑ Spaces
- ☑ Paragraph marks
- ☑ Optional hyphens
- ☑ Hidden text

If you find yourself wondering what each of these characters are, how they are displayed, and what they represent in your document, you will want to review this lesson. Pay particular attention to how you can turn each type of character on and off using the Options selection from the Tools menu.

Section Two

CREATING DOCUMENTS

Documents are the heart of Word for Windows. They contain the ideas and words that you want to develop and print. In this section you will learn how to use documents—how to enter and change text, how to save and load your file, how to print your document, and how to find and replace text. You will use each of these are skills time and again in Word for Windows. By the time you complete this section, you will be able to enter and edit text using the full capabilities of the program.

Lesson 8

Entering and Changing Text

The most fundamental purpose of any word processor is to allow you to enter, edit, and print text. Word for Windows is no different. In addition, however, Word for Windows has many powerful tools that allow you to perform other types of actions in regard to your documents. In this lesson you will learn how Word for Windows enables you to do two of the three fundamental purposes. This lesson covers

- How to enter text
- How to edit what you type
- How to select text
- How to move or copy text

ENTERING YOUR TEXT

When you first start Word for Windows, you will probably see the document window already open and ready for you to enter information, as shown in Figure 8.1:

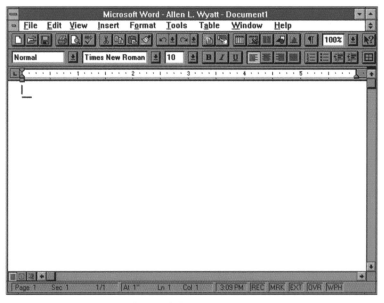

Figure 8.1 New document opened with Word for Windows.

It is possible, however, that your version of Word for Windows doesn't start with an empty document on the screen. If this is the case, simply click on the ▣ tool on the toolbar. This creates a new document window, ready for you to use. Notice the title bar at the top of the document window, or, if your document window is maximized, the title bar at the top of the Word for Windows program window. It indicates a document name, such as Document1, Document2, Document3, or so on. This lets you know you are working with a brand new document—one that has not been given a name yet.

When you have a blank document open, you are ready to begin entering text. All you need to do is to start typing. As you type, Word for Windows displays your text at the position on the screen marked by the blinking cursor. In Word for Windows documentation, this cursor is referred to as the *insertion point*. It marks where your text will be entered. As you type, this cursor moves toward the right. Don't worry about pressing ENTER (as you would on a typewriter). Instead, keep typing as your cursor reaches the right side of the screen and notice what happens. When you finally type something that will no longer fit on the current line, Word for Windows moves the word to the next line. This is called *text wrapping*, or simply *wrapping*.

This feature of Word for Windows—text automatically wrapping at the end of a line—leads to an important point. When you use Word for Windows, you only need to press ENTER at the end of a paragraph. If you have turned on the display of nonprinting characters, as you learned in Lesson 7, your text should *not* appear like Figure 8.2:

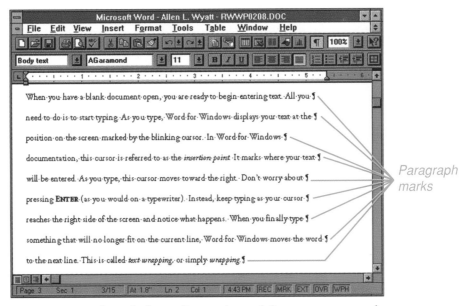

Figure 8.2 Pressing ENTER *at the end of every line, makes each line a new paragraph.*

Instead, your text should appear like Figure 8.3:

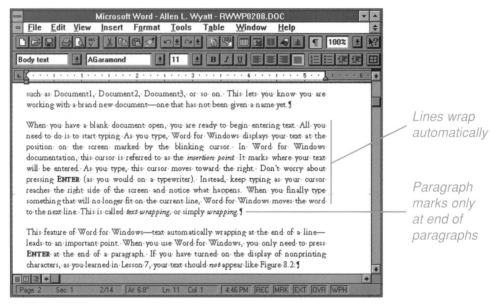

Figure 8.3 Properly entered text.

CHANGING WHAT YOU TYPE

There will come a time when you want to change what you have typed. This changing process is referred to as *editing*. Word for Windows provides many tools that allow you to edit your text. Perhaps one of the simplest (and most often used) editing tools is the BACKSPACE key. Pressing this key moves the cursor toward the left, removing text as it moves. Anything to the right of the cursor remains unchanged. When the cursor reaches the left side of the screen, and you continue pressing the BACKSPACE key, the cursor moves to the previous line.

Using the BACKSPACE key is only suitable for small editing jobs, however. If you want to do anything more extensive, you must use different editing tools. In general, edits in Word for Windows are done by selecting what you want to change and then choosing the function that makes the change. In order to change text, you must first *select* it. Selected text is *highlighted*—light against a dark background, as opposed to the normal dark against a light background.

Selecting the text you want to edit implies that you must be able to move the cursor to the location where you want to make the selection. To move the cursor, you can use either the keyboard or the mouse. You might want to refer back to Lesson 5 to refresh your memory about how to move through your document. Once you have positioned the cursor to where you want to make a selection, you *extend* the cursor. This is done in one of three ways: using the SHIFT key, the **F8** key, or the mouse.

SELECTING TEXT WITH THE SHIFT KEY

With your cursor located at one end of the text you want to select, press and hold down the SHIFT key. As you hold it down, continue to use the cursor control keys. Notice that the cursor expands to include more and more text as you move it. For instance, the words *anything more* are selected in the following:

```
                                    Selected text
Using·the·Backspace·key·is·only·suitable·for·small·editing·jobs,·however.··If·
you·want·to·do·anything·more·extensive,·you·must·use·different·editing·
tools.··In·general,·edits·in·Word·for·Windows·are·done·by·selecting·what·you·
want·to·change,·and·then·choosing·the·function·that·makes·the·change.¶
```

SELECTING TEXT WITH THE F8 KEY

If you don't want to hold down the SHIFT key, you can also use the **F8** key to mark the beginning of a selection. When you do this, the letters EXT (meaning *extension*) appear on the status bar:

```
 Page 1    Sec 1      1/1    At 1"    Ln 1    Col 1      6:11 PM  REC  MRK  EXT  OVR  WPH
```

As you then move the cursor, the selection is extended to include everything between where you pressed **F8** and the current cursor position. To turn off extension mode, simply press an editing key or press ESC.

With the extension mode turned on, you can also perform other tasks that are not possible when you hold down the SHIFT key to make a selection. For instance, you can search for a word (see Lesson 13), and everything between where you pressed **F8**, and the occurrence of what you are searching for will be selected.

SELECTING TEXT WITH THE MOUSE

If you prefer, you can use the mouse to make selections. This is done by moving the mouse cursor so it is positioned at one end of what you want to select. Then press and hold down the left mouse button. As you move the mouse (with the button held down), the selection grows. To end the selection, release the mouse button. (In other words, drag the cursor across the text you want to select.) You can also use the mouse to select a whole word (including the space after, if there is one) by simply double-clicking on the word. If you double-click a word and then, while still holding the mouse button down, drag (forward or backward) across more text, the text will be selected one word at a time, rather than one letter at a time, which can be handy.

If you want to select large amounts of text with the mouse, you can move the mouse cursor into the *selection bar* area. This is a narrow, invisible area to the left of your text. As you move the mouse cursor into this area, it changes to a right-pointing arrow.

If you click on the left mouse button, the line pointed to by the mouse cursor is selected. If you double-click, the entire paragraph is selected. If you hold down the left mouse button and move the mouse, then the selection is extended by either a line or a paragraph at a time.

SELECTING COLUMNS OF TEXT

So far you have learned how to select *contiguous* text. This is a fancy way of saying that the text you select is all next to each other. In other words, you know how to select letters, words, lines, or paragraphs that are all next to each other. There will be times, however, when this type of selection won't suffice. What if you want to select a column of text?

Word for Windows allows you to define a rectangular selection anywhere on the screen. Any text within that rectangle is considered part of the selection, as shown in Figure 8.4:

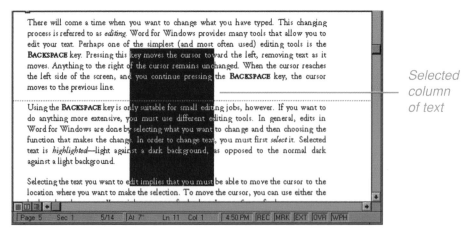

Selected column of text

Figure 8.4 Drag with the right mouse button to select a column.

You can select text in this manner by moving the mouse cursor to one corner of the rectangle. Hold down the ALT key, then press and hold down the left mouse button. As you move the mouse (with the button held down), the rectangular selection area grows. When you release the mouse button, the selection area is set.

You can also use the keyboard to define a rectangular selection area, if desired. To do this, use the SHIFT-CTRL-**F8** combination. Now, as you move the cursor, the selection area grows. To turn off column extension mode, simply press an editing key, press ESC, or press SHIFT-CTRL-**F8** again.

QUICK REVIEW

Word for Windows allows you to make text selections quickly and easily. You can select text either as contiguous blocks or as a rectangular area.

1. To select a block of text, either hold down the SHIFT key and cursor control keys, use the **F8** key to toggle select mode on and off, or hold down the left mouse button and move the mouse to highlight (select) the desired text.

2. To select a rectangular area, hold down the right mouse button and move the mouse, or press SHIFT-CTRL-**F8** to toggle column select mode on and off.

MAKING LARGER EDITS

Once you have selected an block of text, you can edit it in any number of ways. For instance, if you press either BACKSPACE or DEL, then the block is deleted from your document. You can accomplish much the same task by pressing CTRL-**X**. The difference is that CTRL-**X** saves the text on the *Clipboard*, a memory location from which you can then paste it into a new spot, whereas DEL and BACKSPACE do not. Pressing CTRL-**X** is referred to as *cutting* text, while pressing DEL or BACKSPACE is referred to as *clearing* text. The significance of being able to cut text, as opposed to clearing it, will become apparent later in this lesson.

One other feature of Word for Windows is that when you have made a selection, and you then start typing, the information you type *replaces* the selection you have made. This is very powerful, removing the need to clear existing text explicitly before you being typing again. For instance, suppose you have typed a paragraph, and you want to replace the phrase *accomplish much* with the word *perform*. The first thing to do is to select the phrase, using one of the methods learned earlier in this lesson:

of·text,·you·can·edit·it·in·any·nu
either·**Backspace**·or·**Del**,·then·
u·can·accomplish·much·the·same
·is·that·**Ctrl-X**·saves·the·text·on
:**kspace**·do·not.··Pressing·**Ctrl-I**
pressing·**Del**·or·**Backspace**·is·re

*Select text
to replace*

Once selected, just start typing the new phrase. When you press the first key, the selected text is removed and replaced with that single letter. As you continue typing, the new text is inserted into the paragraph.

MOVING AND COPYING TEXT

One common editing task is to move text around in your document, or to copy existing text to a different location in your document. Both of these functions are very closely related to each other. They are accomplished by first selecting the text you want to move or copy, as described earlier in this lesson. Once the text is selected, there are two ways you can move or copy it. One involves the Clipboard, and the other involves using the mouse.

USING THE CLIPBOARD

Earlier you learned that you can use CTRL-X to cut text from your document. This is the cutting part of the process called *cutting and pasting,* which is the same as moving text. Once it is cut, you only need to position the cursor where you want the text moved and press CTRL-V to *paste* (insert) the text at that location.

If you want to copy the text, the process is the same, except that you press CTRL-C instead of CTRL-X. This command copies the selection to the Clipboard, leaving the original. You can then move the cursor and paste the selection wherever you desire.

If you ever forget these commands (**CTRL-V, CTRL-C,** and **CTRL-X**), they are also available as menu choices from the Edit menu:

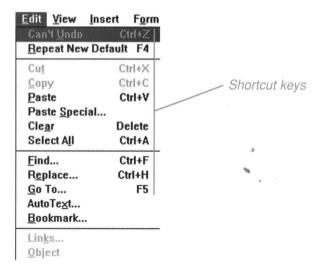

Note that the shortcut keys that are available for an action are shown to the right of that action on the menu.

DRAGGING AND DROPPING

One of the unique features of Word for Windows is the ability to treat a block of text just as any other object on the screen. This means you can use the mouse to move text. For instance, if you have selected a block, you can move the mouse cursor over the top of the selection. When you do, it changes to an arrow. Press and hold down the left mouse button, and the cursor changes again, this time to an arrow with a shadow box below it and a shadow insertion point before it. Continue to hold down the button and move the mouse. When the mouse pointer is located where you want the block moved, release the mouse button. The text is moved to this new location, the quick equivalent of cutting. If you want to move a copy of the selection (it can be as small as a single character) and leave the original behind, hold down the CTRL button until you release the mouse button. This is the quick equivalent of copying.

WHAT YOU NEED TO KNOW

Entering and editing text is the basis of everything you do in Word for Windows. In this lesson you have learned the ground rules that Word for Windows uses in allowing you to enter and edit your text. In particular, you have learned the following fundamental skills:

How to enter text

☑ When to press ENTER

☑ How to edit text

☑ How to make text selections with the keyboard

☑ How to make text selections with the mouse

☑ How to move text with the keyboard

☑ How to copy text with the keyboard

☑ How to move text with the mouse

As you continue to use Word for Windows, these skills will become second nature. Before you know it, you will find it just as easy to change text as it is to enter it in the first place.

Lesson 9

Breaking Your Text

In Lesson 8 you learned how to enter and change text. As part of this learning process, you discovered that you should only press ENTER at the end of a paragraph. Normally, Word for Windows takes care of wrapping text within the margins that are defined for your document. But what if you want a specific line to end before you reach the right margin, and you don't actually want to end your paragraph by pressing ENTER? In this lesson you will learn how to *break* your text. In particular, you will learn how to add the following types of breaks to your document:

- Line breaks

- Page breaks

- Section breaks

You will also learn why each type of break is important and when it should be used.

UNDERSTANDING LINE BREAKS

There may be many times when you want to end a line before you reach the right margin. If the line is the last one of the paragraph, this is no problem—all you need to do is press ENTER. However, there may be times when you don't want to end the paragraph. For instance, the paragraph might be formatted so that pressing ENTER results in an extra line being placed after the paragraph. If you don't want that extra line, you can insert a *line break character* where you want the line to end. This comes in especially handy if you are entering several short lines you want treated as a group, for instance if you are entering an address.

A line break character is entered in your text by pressing SHIFT-ENTER at the point where you want the line broken. If you have turned on the display of nonprinting characters (see Lesson 7), the line break character appears as a backward-pointing arrow. For instance, the following address lines are ended by line break characters:

```
Allen L. Wyatt↵
Discovery Computing, Inc.↵          Line break characters
2323 State Route 585↵
PO Box 738↵                          Paragraph mark
Sundance, WY  82729¶
```

Notice that instead of paragraph marks at the end of the first four lines, there are line break characters. The only place where ENTER was pressed (and a paragraph mark inserted) is at the end of the last address line.

For editing purposes, line break characters are treated the same as any other character. You can select them and change them in the same way as you would a letter or a number. For instance, to delete a line break character, simply position the cursor just before the character and press DEL. Other deletion methods, discussed in Lesson 8, will also work.

UNDERSTANDING PAGE BREAKS

Typically when you are using Word for Windows, the program takes care of paginating your document. *Pagination* is the process of dividing your document into pages, based on the margin settings. Word for Windows calculates how much vertical space each line and paragraph occupies, takes into account the top and bottom page margins, and then breaks your text between pages at the appropriate place, inserting *automatic page breaks*. A page break, when inserted in your document, looks like a thin dotted line extending the entire width of your document, as shown in Figure 9.1:

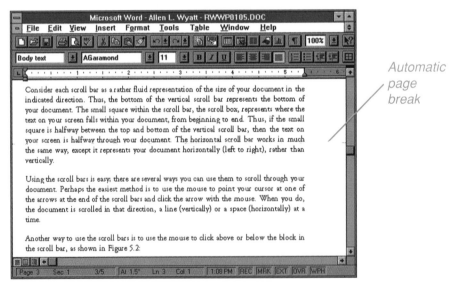

Automatic page break

Figure 9.1 In Normal view, an automatic page break appears as a dotted line.

Note: You won't see page break lines in Page Layout view—instead, the text will start on a new page.

Allowing Word for Windows to control pagination requires no effort on your part. There will be times, however, when you need to start a new page at a different location than would have been chosen by Word for Windows. This is easily done by inserting a *manual page break*. Whenever you insert a page break, everything after the page break will appear at the top of a new page. A manual page break appears within your document as a thin dotted line, but the dots are much closer together than with an automatic page break. In addition, a label is added to the break to indicate its type, as shown in Figure 9.2:

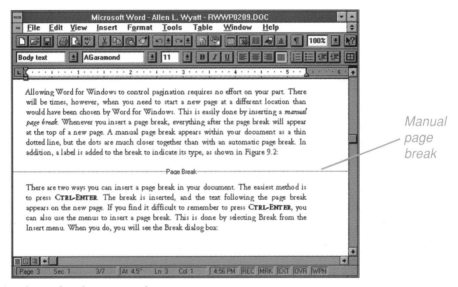

Manual page break

Figure 9.2 Manual page break in Normal view.

There are two ways you can insert a page break in your document. The easiest method is to press CTRL-ENTER. The break is inserted, and the text following the page break appears on the new page. If you find it difficult to remember to press CTRL-ENTER, you can also use the menus to insert a page break. This is done by selecting Break from the Insert menu. When you do, you will see the Break dialog box, as shown in Figure 9.3:

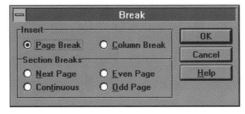

Figure 9.3 Break dialog box.

When this dialog box appears, the Page Break option is always selected. All you need to do is click on the OK button or press ENTER. A page break is inserted in your document at the location of your cursor.

To delete a manual page break, simply delete it as you would any other character. One way to do this is to position the cursor on the page break (on the dotted line) and press the DEL key. You can only delete manual page breaks however. You cannot delete automatic page breaks.

UNDERSTANDING SECTION BREAKS

In Word for Windows, you can divide your document into pieces called *sections*. These sections can be formatted differently from other sections within your document. For instance, one section might be formatted with one-inch margins, while another has two columns and half-inch margins. You will learn more about how to format your document later in this book.

To insert a section break in your document, select Break from the Insert menu. Word for Windows displays the Break dialog box, as shown in Figure 9.4:

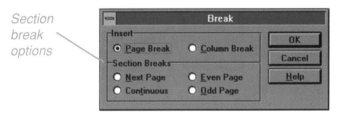

Figure 9.4 Break dialog box.

This dialog box should appear familiar if you read the last section on inserting page breaks. The bottom part of the Break dialog box allows you to insert section breaks. There are four types of section breaks you can specify, as shown here:

- Next page
- Continuous
- Even Page
- Odd Page

The difference between these types of section breaks is the way that Word for Windows treats the section change. It is assumed that any section break signifies a change in page layout or margins. Three of the sections breaks, Next Page, Even Page, and Odd Page, result in Word for Windows beginning the new section formatting at the top of a new page. A Next Page section break starts at the top of the following page, an Even section break starts at the top of the next even-numbered page, and an Odd section break starts at the top of the next odd-numbered page. Both Even Page and Odd Page section breaks result in Word for Windows inserting a blank page in your printout, if necessary.

The Continuous section break causes the next section to begin immediately, wherever the break occurs on the page. This type of section break is used primarily if you want to change layout in the middle of a page. For instance, if you want to mix single- and multicolumn text on one page.

No matter which type of section break you insert in your document, Word for Windows signifies its presence by inserting a dotted double line that extends the full width of your document (dotted lines aren't shown in Page Layout view; instead you see the page as it will be printed). As with the manual page break, Word for Windows includes a label that indicates the existence of the break, as shown in Figure 9.5:

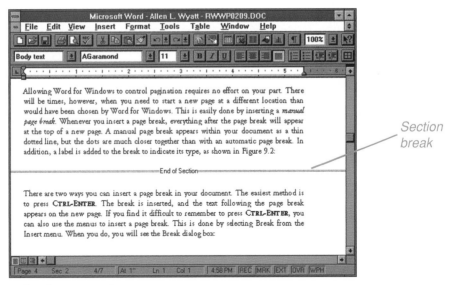

Figure 9.5 Section break in Normal view.

As you move through your document, you will notice that the information on the status bar is updated. At the left of the status bar is an indication of which page number the cursor is located on, followed by which section it is on. As you pass from one section to another, the section number on the status bar is updated to reflect your current position. Sections are always numbered consecutively within a document, starting with Section 1.

You can delete a section break by positioning the cursor on the section break (the dotted double line) and pressing the DEL key. The formatting peculiar to the first section is removed, and the new combined section retains the formatting of the second section.

WHAT YOU NEED TO KNOW

Within Word for Windows, breaks are used to end a line, page, or section prematurely. In this lesson you have learned how:

- ☑ To add line, page, and section breaks
- ☑ To determine when breaks should be used
- ☑ Breaks are noted in your document
- ☑ To delete breaks

If you are a Word for Windows novice, you might not think that breaks are used very often, and perhaps, for your type of documents, they are not. But they are used quite extensively as you start to use Word for Windows to create more and more documents. You should become at least conversant, if not proficient, in their proper use.

Lesson 10

Saving Your Document

Now that you know how to enter and change text, it is time to save your document. Saving documents is an important function. If you don't save them, you can't load them and work on them or print them at a later time. In this lesson, you will focus on how to save your documents, while Lesson 11 covers how to load them. Specifically, this lesson covers

- Commands you can use to save your document

- Different methods of saving a document

- How to automatically save your work

- Forcing Word for Windows to make backup copies of your documents

Word for Windows provides three different commands to save your documents. These commands are available from the File menu:

<u>S</u>ave	Ctrl+S
Save <u>A</u>s...	
Save Al<u>l</u>	

The third option, Save All, only has value if you have multiple files open at the same time. The other two, however, are commands you will use all the time.

THE SAVE COMMAND

The Save option from the File menu is used to save your work to disk. It is effectively the same as clicking on the 🖫 tool from the toolbar. This command does not give you the opportunity to name your file; it simply saves it to disk. If your document is unnamed (you haven't saved your new document yet), the Save command functions the same as the Save As command.

If you are saving a large file, then Word for Windows will display a gauge on the status bar indicating what percentage of the file has been saved.

THE SAVE AS COMMAND

The Save As command is used whenever you want to save your document to a brand new filename or directory. When you choose this command, you will see the Save As dialog box, which appears similar to Figure 10.1:

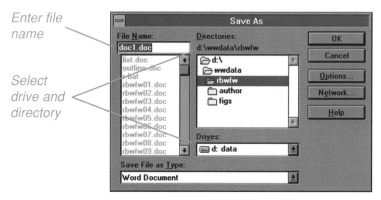

Enter file name

Select drive and directory

Figure 10.1 *Save As dialog box.*

If you are familiar with other Windows products, you will have no problem using this dialog box. All you need to do is change the directory or disk drive (if desired), and specify a filename. By default, Word for Windows document files use the DOC filename extension. When you press ENTER or click on the OK button, your document is saved to the file you specified.

You only need to use the Save As command when you first save a document or when you want to change the filename or directory used for the document. If you are working with a document that has already been saved once, you can just use the Save command. It is much quicker than using the Save As command—it doesn't call up a dialog box.

HOW WORD FOR WINDOWS SAVES DOCUMENTS

Word for Windows uses regular disk files to store your document, but you can control the format used. There are two types of file saving techniques that Word for Windows employs. One is small and the other is fast.

The small technique is so named because it results in the smallest disk files. Every time your file is saved, it is entirely rewritten to disk. If you are working with large or complex documents, this can mean that this saving technique takes a while to complete.

The second technique is called the fast technique, or *Fast Save*. When Word for Windows employs this method, your file is saved once, and then your changes are simply appended to the end of the disk file. Thus, if you work with a large document, Word for Windows saves it the first time and then proceeds to save your edits at the end of the disk file. This is faster than the small technique because only your edits have to be written to disk—not your entire file. This also means, however, that the resulting file is larger than absolutely necessary. This is because the file contains both your original text and the edits. When using Fast Save, Word for Windows will completely rewrite your document file after a certain number of saves. The number of saves after which Word for Windows performs a normal save can vary, based the number of edits you perform and the size of your document.

To control which method Word for Windows will use for saving your documents, choose Options from the Tools menu. You will see the Options dialog box, which appears similar to Figure 10.2:

Click on
Save file
card

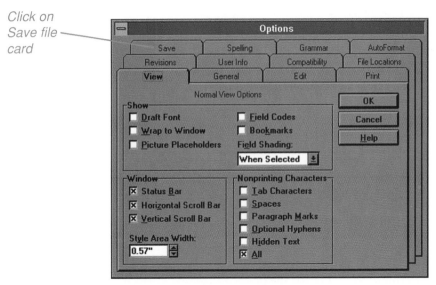

Figure 10.2 *Options dialog box showing View file card.*

The way to use this dialog box has been covered in at least two earlier lessons, so you should be familiar with it by now. Choose the file card labeled Save. The Options dialog box will now display the options related to how Word for Windows saves your document, as shown in Figure 10.3:

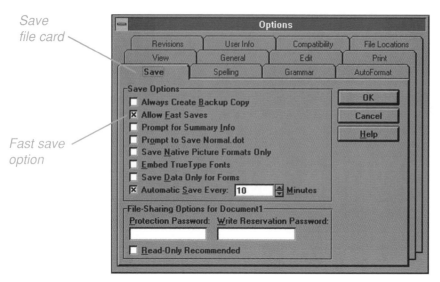

Figure 10.3 Options dialog box showing Save file card.

To enable Fast Save, make sure an   appears in the check box for the *Allow Fast Saves* option. If you later decide you don't want to use Fast Saving, simply clear the check box by again clicking on it with the mouse pointer.

AUTOMATICALLY SAVING YOUR WORK

If you sit at your computer and use Word for Windows for hours on end, you know it is easy to get so wrapped up in your work that you forget to save your document. This can be very dangerous, since you could lose your work if the power goes out or the program freezes for some reason. (One of the corollaries to Murphy's law states that the power will always go out 15 seconds before you save your document.)

Word for Windows allows you to save your document automatically, at any interval you desire. Thus, you will not need to remember to save your work. Instead, you can concentrate on the content of your document.

To instruct Word for Windows to automatically save your work, choose Options from the Tools menu. Choose the file card labeled Save. The Options dialog box will appear similar to Figure 10.4:

Save
file card

Automatic
save option

Save interval

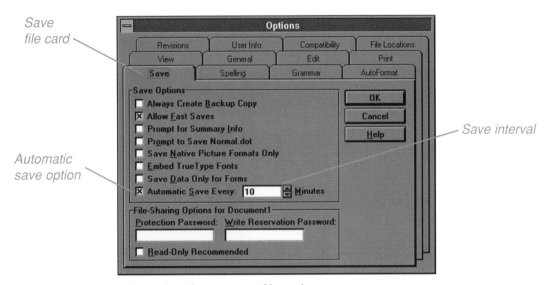

Figure 10.4 Options dialog box showing Save file card.

To enable automatic saving, make sure an   appears in the check box for the Automatic Save option. The control box should then display the number of minutes after which Word for Windows will save your work. This is an interval time period and represents how frequently your work is saved. If you want to use a different interval, simply change the number using either the up and down arrows to the right of the number, or by entering a number with the keyboard. You can specify any interval between one minute and 120 minutes (two hours).

KEEPING BACKUP COPIES OF YOUR WORK

Backup copies, by definition, are simply the file as it was previously saved. Thus, if you save your document, the old document file is renamed to have the BAK extension, and the current document is saved in the document file with the DOC extension. In this way you always have at least one older generation of your document to fall back upon, if necessary.

The only problem with making backup copies of your documents is that they can occupy quite a bit of disk space. If you have backup copies for all your documents, you effectively double the amount of disk space necessary for the files. Many people find this unacceptable, so Word for Windows, by default, does not make backup copies of your documents. If you want to force Word for Windows to make backup copies, you should choose Options from the Tools menu. Make sure that the file card labeled Save is selected. The Options dialog box will appear similar to Figure 10.5:

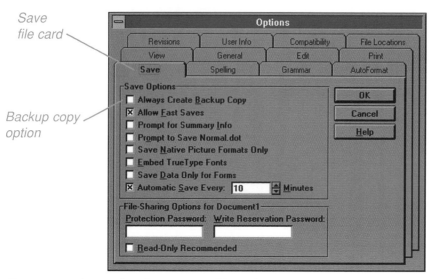

Figure 10.5 *Options box showing Save file card.*

The first option on the dialog box is Always Create Backup Copy. Ensure that there is an　in the check box to the left of this option, and Word for Windows will make backup copies every time you save your document. You should note that you cannot choose both Fast Save and Always Create Backup Copy. Word for Windows will allow you to only do one or the other.

WHAT YOU NEED TO KNOW

Word for Windows provides many different ways you can save your documents. When you are using the program, sooner or later you will need to save your work. (This is, of course, unless you don't care about saving your documents after each work session.)

In this lesson you have learned the following:

- ☑ Saving frequently will prevent a lot of pain.
- ☑ You use the Save As command to save a new file or save an existing file to a new name or directory.
- ☑ You use the Save command to save recent changes to a previously saved file.
- ☑ You can save documents in two ways—normal and Fast Save.
- ☑ You can instruct Word for Windows to save your work at set intervals.

Once you have saved your document, the assumption is that you will need to load (open) it again. Loading your documents is covered in Lesson 11.

Lesson 11

Loading Your Document

In Lesson 10 you learned how to save your document. One of the inherent strengths of a word processor is the ability to save and, at a later time, reload your documents. In this lesson you will learn

- How to load your Word for Windows documents
- How to load different types of files
- How to search for files

LOADING A WORD FOR WINDOWS DOCUMENT

In Word for Windows, loading a document is referred to as *opening a document* or *opening a file.* This is done in one of two ways. First, you can use the Open command from the File menu. Second, you can use the 🖼 tool on the toolbar. No matter which method you use to load a file, you will see the Open dialog box, as shown in Figure 11.1:

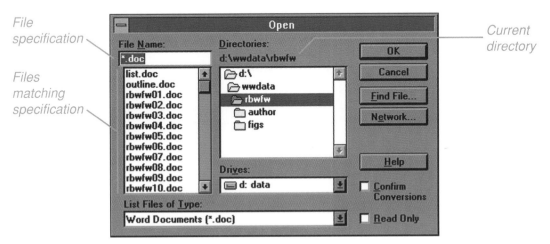

File specification

Files matching specification

Current directory

Figure 11.1 Open dialog box.

If you are familiar with any other Windows programs that use files, this dialog box might look familiar. The simplest way to use it is to just select a document file and press ENTER or click on the OK button. Alternatively, you could simply double-click on the filename. If desired, you can specify other directories or disk drives from which you wish to load a document.

When you instruct Word for Windows to load a file, it reads the file contents into memory so you can either edit or print the file. The original file remains on the disk; it is not changed. Any changes you make occur only in the computer's memory. You should remember to save any changes (as you learned in Lesson 10) if you want those changes to be permanent.

SELECTING OTHER FILES

By default, Word for Windows displays only document files when you choose to open a file. Document files have a filename extension of DOC. However, you can also instruct Word for Windows to load different types of files. There are two ways to do this.

The simplest method is to specify a different file type in the List Files of Type field at the bottom of the Open dialog box. When you click on the arrow to the right of this field, you will see a list of commonly used files that Word for Windows understands, as shown in Figure 11.2:

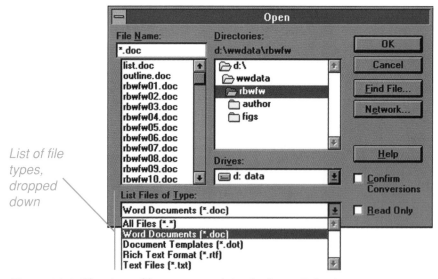

List of file types, dropped down

Figure 11.2 Choosing a file type to match in the Open dialog box.

Select one of these, and Word for Windows displays only those types of files in the file list. If you instruct Word for Windows to display all files, you will see all files in the current directory.

The other way to view different files is to enter a file specification in the File Name field at the top of the file list. This is essentially all that Word for Windows does. It displays all the document files when the file specification is set to *.DOC. If you choose to display all the files in the directory, then the file specification is set to *.*. You can use any file specification you desire.

The file specification you use must adhere to DOS file specification rules. This means that you can use any legal filename characters, along with the question mark (?) and asterisk (*) wildcard characters. The question mark is used as a placeholder for a single character, while an asterisk is used as a placeholder one or more characters. If you need additional information on wildcard characters, you may want to refer to the book *Rescued by DOS,* Jamsa Press, 1993.

Once you have displayed the file list as you like it (by using the two methods just described), you can load a specific file using the same steps covered in the previous section.

QUICKLY LOADING YOUR MOST RECENT DOCUMENTS

Many people who work with Word for Windows work with the same documents over and over again. For instance, you might be working on a report for work or school, and that work covers a period of several weeks. Every time you use Word for Windows, you load this same file and continue working and refining your thoughts. If you find yourself in this situation, it is bothersome to repeatedly go through the steps to open the file.

Word for Windows provides a shortcut you can use to sidestep this hassle. Take a look at the File menu, as shown in Figure 11.3:

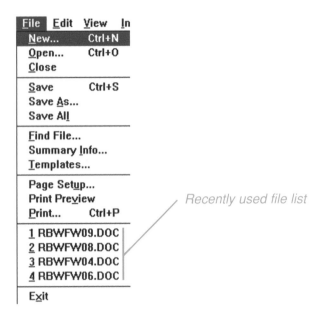

Figure 11.3 File menu.

Notice that there are four files listed at the bottom of the menu. These are the four most recent files that you have loaded (number 1 being the most recent). Thus, they represent the last work you did with Word for Windows. If you want to load a file you used in your previous Word for Windows session, you can simply pull down the File menu and select the file you want to use. From the keyboard, you can press ALT-F and then the number to the left of the file you want.

FINDING YOUR FILES

As you work with Word for Windows over an extended period, it is possible to create many, many files. You might have letters, reports, memos, and a myriad of other documents stored on your hard drive. Chances are that you have several versions of some of these documents. If you haven't worked with a document in a while, it is very easy to forget the document's filename. So how do you locate it again?

The easiest way is to use the Find File capability built into Word for Windows. This can be accessed in one of two ways. First, you can select Find File from the File menu. Second, you can click on the Find File button on the Open dialog box (shown earlier in this lesson).

The dialog box you see next depends on whether you have used the Find File feature before. If you have not, you will see the Search dialog box in Figure 11.4:

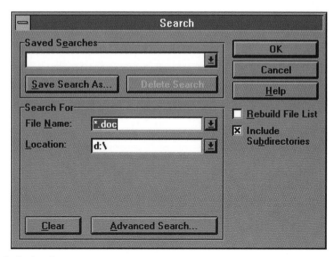

Figure 11.4 Search dialog box.

If you have, you are taken directly to the Find File dialog box (discussed shortly) and shown the results of your last file search. Click on the Search button to bring up the Search dialog box. The Find File feature of Word for Windows is very powerful. You can use it to search for files in a specific drive or directory. Explaining the full use of this feature is far beyond the scope of this book. However, it is helpful for you to know how to use Find File to look for a document.

Only a few fields in the Search dialog box are of any consequence when doing a simple file search. Word for Windows allows you to perform much more detailed searches, however, by clicking on the Advanced Search dialog box. You won't need to do that most of the time, and there is no need to do it right now. For most searches, you can simply fill in the information on this dialog box.

The most commonly used fields on the Search dialog box are the File Name and Location fields. In the File Name field you can provide a file specification, using the same techniques as you learned earlier in this lesson. In the Location field you indicate where you want Word for Windows to search. When you click on the arrow to the right of the Location field, you can select individual drives or directories you want to search.

As an example of how to use Find File quickly, let's suppose you want to search drive C for all of your document files. Enter *.**DOC** in the File Name field and choose **C:** in the Location field. To search all directories on drive C, select the check box to the left of the Include Subdirectories label.

When you have finished providing the search specification, click on the OK button. Word for Windows reads through the drives and directories you have specified, looking for files that meet your criteria. These files are then displayed in the Find File dialog box, as shown in Figure 11.5:

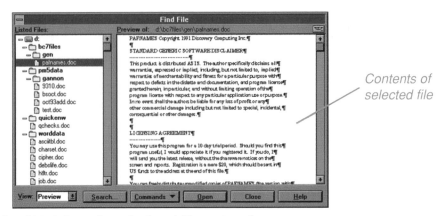

Figure 11.5 Results of *.DOC search, with selected file previewed.

Notice that the left side of the Find File dialog box displays a list of files located in the search, regardless of which directory they were located within. To the right side of the dialog box is information about the highlighted file. You can control which information is shown in this part of the dialog box by clicking on the View field. Chances are you will want the content of your files displayed. If the file is a Word for Windows document, the display looks just like a miniature version of the document.

You can display different files by using the arrow keys or the mouse to select different files from the file list. You can then browse through these files and perform other searches, as desired. When you have located the file you want, click on ▐ **Open** ▌, and Word for Windows will open the file for you.

WHAT YOU NEED TO KNOW

This lesson has covered a lot of ground, particularly in the last section. Word for Windows allows you to load all types of documents—even those that were not created by Word for Windows. In this lesson you have learned how to

- ☑ Load a Word for Windows document
- ☑ Load a different type of document
- ☑ Load your most recently edited documents
- ☑ Find a document on your hard disk

These skills, particularly the skill of finding lost files, are extremely useful when using Word for Windows. You will need to practice finding files, but over time you will be able to use the loading features of Word for Windows with no problem at all.

Lesson 12

Printing Your Document

A word processor (Word for Windows included) would be of little value if it did not allow you to print your documents. Printing is, typically, the end result of any document you create. This lesson provides you with the information you need in order to

- Select your printer

- Use Print Preview to see your document before printing it

- Print your document easily and quickly

- Print a single copy of your document

SETTING UP YOUR PRINTER

Word for Windows works with whatever printers you have set up in Windows. Adding printer drivers and configuring Windows to work with your printers is beyond the scope of this book. However, you might want to refer to *Rescued by Windows,* Jamsa Press, 1993, for more information in this area.

One of the important things you can do with Word for Windows is to make sure you have the proper printer selected for your output. If you have only one printer, this step will not be necessary. Only when you have installed more than one printer driver with Windows will you need to do this.

To specify which printer you want Word for Windows to use, select Print from the File menu. You will then see the Print dialog box, as shown in Figure 12.1:

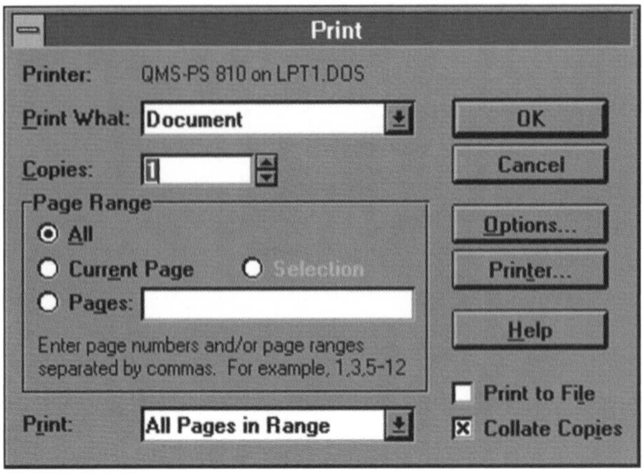

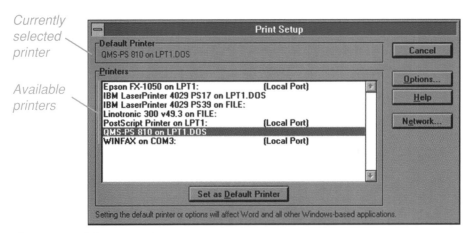

Figure 12.1 *Print dialog box.*

From this dialog box, you should choose the [Printer...] button. This results in the display of the Print Setup dialog box, similar to Figure 12.2:

Currently selected printer

Available printers

Figure 12.2 *Selecting a printer.*

The list of printers shown in your dialog box will differ from those shown here, but they will match the printers you have defined within Windows. Highlight the printer you want to use and then click on [Set as Default Printer]. The Default Printer, listed at the top of the dialog box, will change to the printer you selected. When you are satisfied with your printer selection, click on [Cancel]. You are returned to the Print dialog box.

USING PRINT PREVIEW

How many times have you printed a document, only to find some little thing wrong? You make the correction and print again. In some instances, you might print the same document several times before it is just right. Word for Windows provides a tool you can use so you don't have to waste so much paper in producing your final output. This tool is called Print Preview.

When you choose the Print Preview option from the File menu, or use the 🔍 tool from the Standard toolbar, what you see on your screen will change significantly. Any toolbars and the ruler will disappear (to provide more screen space), and you will see an exact representation of how your printed document will look, as shown in Figure 12.3:

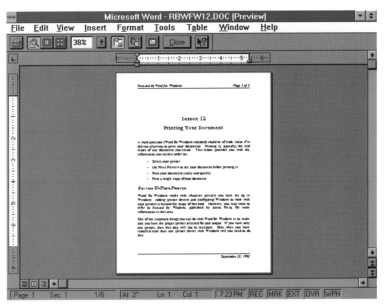

Figure 12.3 Print Preview.

Notice that a new toolbar, specific to Print Preview, appears at the top of your screen. The tools on this toolbar allow you to control what you see (one or multiple pages) and make adjustments in margins and layout. You can page through your document by pressing the PGUP or PGDN keys on your keyboard or using the scroll bars. When you have finished and you want to return to normal editing, press ESC or click on the Close button.

The legibility and value of the Print Preview tool will depend, in large part, on the quality and size of the monitor you are using with your computer. If you have a larger monitor and you are using

Windows in a high resolution, then you might be able to read most of the type on the Print Preview display. If you are using a smaller monitor at a lower resolution, however, you will probably only be able to make out the largest headlines in your document.

SENDING YOUR DOCUMENT TO THE PRINTER

When it is finally time to print your document, you do this by using the Print option from the File menu. You will then see the Print dialog box, as shown in Figure 12.4:

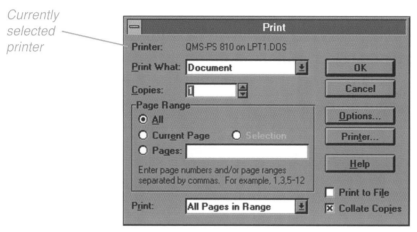

Figure 12.4 Print dialog box.

Note that the information at the top of this dialog box indicates where your document will be printed. If this is not the printer you want to use, choose a different printer, as described earlier in this lesson.

The actual information and options available from the Print dialog box can vary, depending on the type of printer you are using. Different printers have different capabilities, and Windows takes advantage of these capabilities as much as possible. In general, however, you can use this dialog box to select the number of copies you want to print, along with which pages you want to print.

One of the other things you can specify is what you want sent to the printer. This is done using the Print What field. By default, this field is set to Document, meaning that only your document will be printed. By changing this field, you can also select any of the following information to be printed:

- Summary info

- Annotations

- Styles

- AutoText entries

- Key assignments

This information reflects settings and customization you can make elsewhere within Word for Windows. You will learn about many of these as you work through the lessons in this book.

When you are satisfied with what you want to print, click on the ⬛ OK ⬛ button or press ENTER. Word for Windows will send your information to the printer, as you have directed.

PRINTING A SINGLE COPY OF YOUR DOCUMENT QUICKLY

Most of the time, you will want to print only one copy of your document. Word for Windows provides a quick way you can do this, using the 🖨 tool. When you click on this button, it is the same as choosing the Print command from the File menu and immediately clicking on OK.

Using the 🖨 tool results in one copy of your entire document being printed. If you need more than one copy, or if you want to print only a portion of your document, you must use the Print command as described in the previous section.

WHAT YOU NEED TO KNOW

Printing your document is a particular strength of Word for Windows. This is because the program makes extensive and effective use of the printer drivers built into Windows. Once you have selected your printer, printing your document is very quick and easy. In this lesson you have learned some of the techniques you can use to print your document. The skills you should have learned include these:

- ☑ How to select your printer

- ☑ How to use the Print Preview feature of Word for Windows

- ☑ How to print your document

- ☑ How to print additional information besides your document

- ☑ How to print a single copy of your document

Lesson 13

Finding and Replacing Text

One of the most common editing tasks you will perform is either searching for text or searching for it and then replacing it with something else. Word for Windows provides powerful tools to perform both functions. In this lesson you will learn

- How to search for text

- How to use special characters in your searches

- How to replace text

SEARCHING FOR TEXT

To search for text, you use the Find option from the Edit menu. When you choose this option, you will see the Find dialog box, as shown in Figure 13.1:

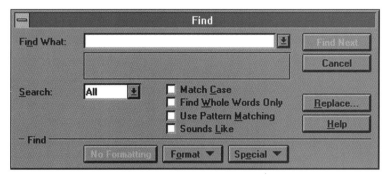

Figure 13.1 Find dialog box.

There are two major parts to this dialog box. The upper part of the dialog box allows you to specify the text you are searching for, along with the direction in which Word for Windows should search. The bottom part is where you can indicate that you want to search for text with specific attributes. There are three buttons:

No Formatting	Clears any formatting attributes you may have specified
Format ▼	Allows you to specify formatting attributes to search for
Special ▼	Allows you to specify special control characters to search for

You will learn more about formatting and character attributes later in this book, so searching for formats will not be covered in this lesson. Suffice it to say, however, that Word for Windows allows you to search for formatting attributes either with or without text. Thus, for instance, you can easily locate all the text in your document that is bold. You can also find all instances of a specific word when that word appears in italics. There are a great many combinations of both text and formatting that make the search capabilities very powerful.

To begin searching for text, you must first enter the text that you want Word for Windows to locate. In the Find What field, enter the text. How you enter the text (upper or lowercase) does not matter, unless you select Match Case. If you do, then Word for Windows will only find the text you specify if it is also the same case as the text you entered. For example, let's assume you are looking for the word *boxes*. If, in the Find What field, you enter **BOXES,** and Match Case is not selected, Word for Windows will consider *boxes*, *Boxes*, *BOXES*, and *BoXes* all as matches. However, if you click on the Match Case button, Word for Windows will ignore all instances of the word except when all the letters are in uppercase. Thus, only *BOXES* would be found.

Notice that right below Match Case is another option—Find Whole Words Only. If you select this option, Word for Windows will return a match only if the text that is found is a whole word. For example, if you were searching for a word such as *the,* and you did not turn on the Find Whole Words Only button, any of the following words could be considered matches:

the	these	theater
bother	mother	Athens

Actually, the entire words would not be matches; just the letters t-h-e contained within each word. The number of words that could be matched is very large, indeed. If the same search were conducted with the Find Whole Words Only option selected, only the word *the* would be matched; all the others would be ignored, because the letters t-h-e contained within them do not constitute whole words.

Finally, in the Search field you can choose whether you want to search the entire document (All), forward (Down) from the current cursor position, or backward (Up) from the current cursor position. If you choose Down or Up, and you do not start searching from the beginning or end of a document, Word for Windows will ask if you want to keep searching from the other end of the document once the beginning or end is reached. Whenever possible, you will want to search forward, particularly if you are working with a large document. Word for Windows performs forward searches a bit faster than backward searches.

Once you have specified what you want to search for and how you want the search to be conducted, click on [Find Next] or press ENTER. The text, if it can be located, is selected and displayed on the screen. The Find dialog box remains visible, and you can continue to search by continually selecting [Find Next]. When you have located the text occurrence you are looking for, you can either click on [Cancel] or press the ESC key.

QUICK REVIEW   *SEARCHING FOR TEXT*

Word for Windows provides a powerful search function that you can use to find any combination of text, formatting, or both within your document. To search for text, follow these steps:

1.   Select Find from the Edit menu.

2.   Specify what you want to find in the Find What field.

3.   Specify how you want it found by using the Match Whole Word Only, Match Case, and Search fields.

4.   Click on the [Find Next] button.

REPLACING TEXT

Now that you know how to search for text, it is a simple task to replace it with new text. The first step is to select the Replace option from the Edit menu. You will then see the Replace dialog box, as shown in Figure 13.2:

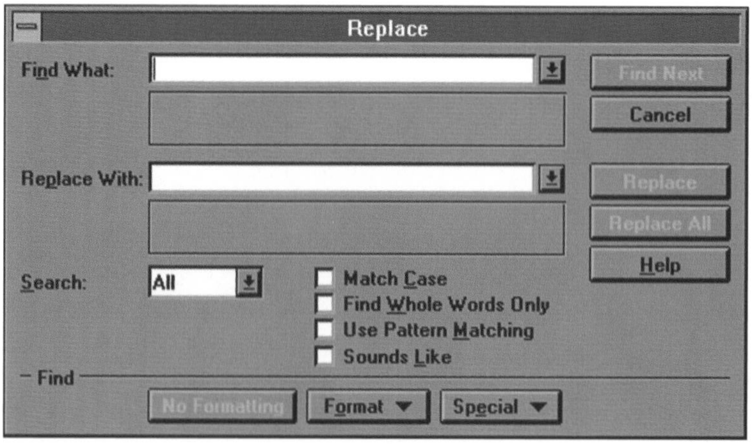

Figure 13.2 Replace dialog box.

This dialog box is similar to the Find dialog box, except there is a new field and two new buttons. The Replace With field is where you can indicate the text you want Word for Windows to use to replace the text it finds. The [Replace] button can be used when the search text is located to indicate that this one instance should be replaced. The [Replace All] button is used to instruct Word for Windows to stop asking and replace all occurrences of the search text.

Earlier in this chapter you learned how to specify what you want Word for Windows to find. When you are using the Replace dialog box, you specify both the Find What and Replace With fields using the same methods described earlier.

SPECIAL CHARACTERS

You probably noticed the [Special ▼] button at the bottom of both the Find and Replace dialog boxes. Word for Windows allows you to both search and replace special characters—those you can't normally see or type on the keyboard. When you select the [Special ▼] button, you can search for or replace with special characters. All you need to do is select the character from the list presented.

You can also enter the special search or replace codes directly, however. These codes are denoted by entering a caret, which is created by pressing SHIFT-6 (caret), followed by a code character. For instance, if you wanted to search or replace a tab character, you would enter ^t within your search or replace field. Some special characters may not be used in the Replace With field. The following are the special characters you can search for:

Characters	Meaning	Search For	Replace With
^#	Any single digit	Yes	No
^$	Any single letter	Yes	No
^&	The search text	No	Yes
^+	Em dash	Yes	Yes
^-	Optional hyphen	Yes	Yes
^=	En dash	Yes	Yes
^?	Any single character	Yes	No
^^	Caret character	Yes	Yes
^~	Nonbreaking hyphen	Yes	Yes
^a	Annotation mark	Yes	No
^b	Section break	Yes	No

Table 13.1 Special Find and Replace characters. (continued on next page)

Characters	Meaning	Search For	Replace With
^c	Clipboard contents	No	Yes
^d	Field	Yes	No
^e	Endnote mark	Yes	No
^f	Footnote	Yes	No
^g	Graphic	Yes	No
^l	Line break	Yes	Yes
^m	Manual page break	Yes	Yes
^n	Column break	Yes	Yes
^p	Paragraph mark	Yes	Yes
^s	Nonbreaking space	Yes	Yes
^t	Tab character	Yes	Yes
^w	White space (any spaces, tabs, breaks, paragraph marks, etc.)	Yes	No

Table 13.1 Special Find and Replace characters. (continued from previous page)

Notice that all the characters following the caret are lowercase. They must be lowercase. As an example of how to use these types of special characters, let's assume you want to search for any paragraphs that begin with the word *While*. This would be done by entering your search text as **^pWhile** and selecting the Match Case option. The leading ^p ensures that Word for Windows will locate only those occurrences of *While* that appear right after the end of a paragraph, meaning they are at the beginning of a new one.

There is one special replacement option that requires a bit more explanation. When you use ^& in the replacement text, the search text is substituted for it when a replacement is done. For instance, let's assume you are searching for *Jamsa* and you want to replace it with *Jamsa Press*. You could specify the full spellings in their respective fields of the Replace dialog box, or you could specify **Jamsa** in the Find What field and **^& Press** in the Replace With field. The ^& is replaced with the search text (*Jamsa*), resulting in *Jamsa Press* being the replacement.

WHAT YOU NEED TO KNOW

This lesson has provided information you can use to both search for and replace text. Before proceeding to the next lesson, make sure you can do the following:

- ☑ Search for text
- ☑ Use special characters in your search
- ☑ Replace text
- ☑ Use special characters in your replacement text

Once you feel comfortable with these skills, you will have mastered the editing tools within Word for Windows. You are now ready to focus on formatting skills.

Section Three

BASIC FORMATTING SKILLS

Formatting refers to the process of adjusting the appearance of your text. Word for Windows allows you to completely separate content (your text) from appearance (the format of your text). You can change and rechange how your text appears until you are completely satisfied with the overall appearance of your document. Word for Windows lets you change the formatting at the character level, paragraph level, and document level. This section will teach you how you can make your document look the best it can.

Lesson 14

Page Layout

The first step in formatting your document is to decide how you want the text to appear in relation to the page. This is referred to as *page layout*. In this lesson you will learn how you can specify and control the following in Word for Windows:

- Page size
- Page orientation
- Page margins
- Number of columns

SETTING PAGE SIZE

In Word for Windows, *page size* means the physical size of the paper on which you will print your document. In most cases, this will be a standard size, such as letter size or legal size. In many cases, the limits on your page size are often determined by your printer.

To set page size within Word for Windows, select the Page Setup option from the File menu. When you do, you will see the Page Setup dialog box. The information displayed in this dialog box is determined by which type of page attributes you choose. For the purposes of this section, choose the Paper Size file card. The dialog box will then look like Figure 14.1:

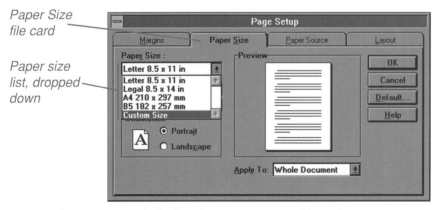

Figure 14.1 Page Setup dialog box showing Paper Size file card.

There are three settings here that are used to define page size. The Paper Size field at the top-left corner of the dialog box allows you choose one of the standard paper sizes. To see which sizes are available, click on the arrow to the right of the field. When you do, you will see a list of standard sizes:

Size	Dimensions
Letter	8.5" 11"
Legal	8.5" 14"
A4	210 mm 297 mm
B5	182 mm 257 mm
Custom Size	Up to you

Table 14.1 *Paper sizes.*

The final option, Custom Size, is used to define your own paper size. For instance, you might have some index cards (3 5) in your printer. Word for Windows allows you to set the page size to this size. You do this by changing the values in the Width and Height fields. You can use widths and heights up to 22 inches.

As you change the page size, notice that the sample page shown at the right of the dialog box also changes to show how your text will appear. When you have finished setting the page size, you can click on the [OK] button.

Note: *At the bottom of the Page Setup window, you will see the Apply To drop-down list, which, when dropped down, contains two settings to control which parts of the document to apply your settings to: Whole Document and This Point Forward. Like the Preview window, this appears in several different Page Setup file cards.*

SETTING PAGE ORIENTATION

Once you have specified the size of your paper, you can indicate how you want Word for Windows to print on it. This is called *page orientation*, and represents how the type appears in relation to the page. There are two different page orientations: *portrait* and *landscape*. Portrait orientation is where the paper is taller than it is wide. Landscape orientation is the opposite.

To set page orientation, choose the Page Setup option from the File menu. When you do, you will see the Page Setup dialog box, as shown earlier in this lesson. Make sure you have selected the Paper Size file card from those available in the Page Setup dialog box.

Near the left-center portion of the dialog box is another box labeled Orientation. The two buttons in this box determine whether Word for Windows will use portrait or landscape orientation. Click on the appropriate button. Each time you choose an orientation, the sample page at the right side of the Page Setup dialog box changes to show how your page will appear.

Note: *If you have changed the page orientation in Word for Windows and you actually want to print in the changed orientation, you must also change the page orientation in the Printers section of the Windows Control Panel.*

When you have finished setting the page orientation, you can click on the [OK] button.

QUICK REVIEW   *SETTING PAGE SIZE AND ORIENTATION*

Page size and orientation determine the type of paper you are using, and how Word for Windows will print upon it. To set page size and orientation, follow these steps:

1. Choose the Page Setup option from the File menu.

2. Choose the Paper Size file card.

3. In the fields provided, specify both the page dimensions and the print orientation.

4. Click on [OK]

You can change page size and orientation at any time you desire.

SETTING PAGE MARGINS

In Word for Windows, page margins are used to determine how much white space (blank area) should be left around your text. Margins are used to provide a visual border for your printed page, and they provide an area where the page can be held or bound.

To set margins, choose the Page Setup option from the File menu. Make sure that the Margins file card is selected. Word for Windows then displays the current margins for your document, as shown in Figure 14.2:

Margins
file card

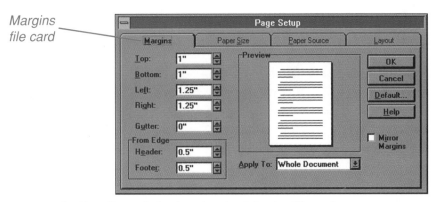

Figure 14.2 Page Setup dialog box showing Margins file card.

Notice that there are five margins you can specify: top, bottom, left, right, and gutter. If you have selected the Mirror Margins check box at the right side of the dialog box, the left and right margins are referred to as inside and outside margins.

Each margin refers to the distance from the edge of the paper to where text begins. Thus, a one-inch top margin means that there will be one inch of white space at the top of each page of your document. You should note, however, that headers and footers (described in Lesson 19) can be printed within the top and bottom margins.

The fifth margin, the *gutter,* might seem unfamiliar to some readers. This margin defines how much extra space should be left on either the left side of each page (or the inside of each page, if you are using Mirror Margins) for binding. Thus, if you are going to three-hole punch your final document, and the punch holes extend 1/2 inch into the paper, you can set a gutter margin of 1/2 inch. Remember that the gutter margin is always in addition to the left (or inside) margin. Thus, if you have a gutter margin of 1/2 inch and a left (or inside) margin of one inch, your total left (or inside) margin will be 1 1/2 inches.

As you change page margins, notice that the sample page at the right side of the dialog box also changes. When you have finished making changes, click on the OK button.

WORKING WITH COLUMNS

Every reader is, no doubt, familiar with columns. This book is written in single-column format. A newspaper, on the other hand, might be written in four- or five-column format. Word for Windows allows you to change easily how many columns you will use in your page layout, as well as how much space you want to leave between each column.

Whenever you divide your document into columns, Word for Windows makes each column the same size. This is done by determining the width of your printed page, subtracting the space between columns, and then dividing the remainder by the number of columns. For instance, let's assume you wanted to use four columns in your document, each separated by . You are using letter-size paper (8.5 11) and you have one-inch left and right margins. The printable area of your paper is 6 1/2 inches (8 1/2 minus 2 for the left and right margins). When you subtract 1 1/2 (the three white spaces between columns are 1/2 inch each), that leaves 5 inches printable. Divide this by the four columns, and each column will be 1 1/4 inches wide.

There are two ways you can change the number of columns in your document. The first is to use the ▦ tool on the toolbar. When you click on this, you will see a small display that indicates a number of columns:

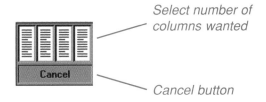

Select number of columns wanted

Cancel button

You simply select the number of columns you want in your document. For instance, if you want your document to use three columns, you would click on the third column. Your document is then divided as you directed.

You can also set up your columns by selecting Columns from the Format menu. When you do, you will see the Columns dialog box, as shown in Figure 14.3:

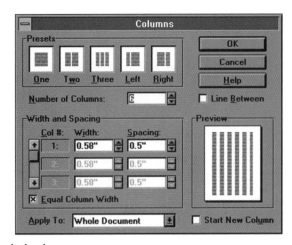

Figure 14.3 Columns dialog box.

Here you can specify exactly how many columns you want to use, as well as how much space to leave between columns and whether to have a line drawn between columns. As you make changes, these changes are reflected in the sample document at the right side of the dialog box.

When you have finished setting up the column layout in your document, click on the [OK] button.

WHAT YOU NEED TO KNOW

In this lesson you have learned the fundamentals of formatting. All formatting begins with how your page appears. Before proceeding to the next chapter, you should make sure you understand the following:

- ☑ How to set page size
- ☑ How to set page orientation
- ☑ How to set text margins
- ☑ What the gutter margin is
- ☑ How to format your text for different numbers of columns

Once you understand these items, you are ready to tackle different types of formatting issues.

Lesson 15

Changing How Paragraphs Look

Now that you know how to specify how your document appears in relation to the actual paper (see Lesson 14), it is time to refine your formatting skills. The place to begin this is with paragraph formatting. In Word for Windows, paragraph formatting consists of the following attributes, which you will learn about in this lesson:

- Alignment
- Indentation
- Pagination
- Spacing

ALIGNING A PARAGRAPH

In most any word processing programs, there are three ways you can align text: left, center, and right. Left-aligned text has all characters moved as far left on the line as possible, with the right end falling as it will (ragged right). Center-aligned (or simply centered) text has equal amounts of white space on both the left and right side of the line. Right-aligned text (as you might expect) has all the characters moved as far right as possible, letting the left be ragged.

Word for Windows, on the other hand, includes a fourth type of alignment. This type goes by several different names—fill alignment, justified, or fill-justified. Whatever the name, however, the result is the same. With this type of alignment, all the lines within a paragraph are expanded so both the left and right margins are even.

There are two ways you can align paragraphs within Word for Windows. The first (and easiest) is to use the alignment buttons on the formatting toolbar. When you click on one of these buttons, any paragraphs you have selected (or the paragraph that your cursor is currently in) are aligned in that way. There are four such buttons, shown in Table 15.1:

Button	Meaning
	Left alignment
	Center alignment
	Right alignment
	Justified alignment

Table 15.1 *Paragraph alignment buttons in Word for Windows.*

The other method for setting paragraph alignment is to use the Paragraph option from the Format menu. When you choose this option, make sure you have the Indents and Spacing file card selected, and you will see the Paragraph dialog box, as shown in Figure 15.1:

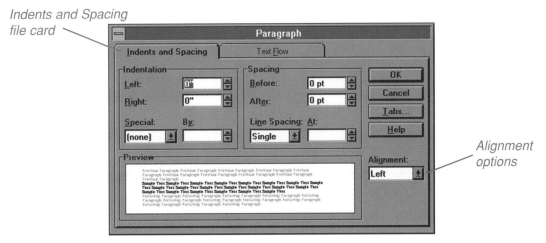

Figure 15.1 *Paragraph dialog box showing Indents and Spacing file card.*

In the lower-right corner of this dialog box is a box (a drop-down list) labeled Alignment. When you click on the arrow to the right of the field, you can see the four alignment choices. After you have selected one of them, you can click on OK to make the choice effective.

INDENTING A PARAGRAPH

Indenting a paragraph determines how much additional space you want to leave on either the left or right sides of the paragraph. This indentation is in addition to the left and right margin indentations, which you learned how to set in Lesson 14, "Page Layout."

There are three ways you can change the paragraph indentation. You can use the indentation tools on the toolbar, use the menus, or use the ruler. The first two methods will be covered in this section, with the third being deferred to the following section.

The first method for changing paragraph indention is to use the indentation tools on the Formatting toolbar. These tools allow you to change only the indentation of the left margin, however. The 📑 tool moves the paragraph to the left, and the 📑 tool moves it to the right. Each click of the tool moves it further in the direction indicated.

While the indentation tools might be good for rough moves, they won't suffice when you need more precision or when you want to change the right indentation. In these instances, you need to use the Paragraph option from the Format menu. This option results in the Paragraph dialog box being displayed, as shown earlier in this lesson. At the left side of the dialog box is a box labeled Indentation. In this box are three fields, which control how the paragraph is indented. The Left and Right settings control the indentation of the left and right sides of the paragraph. The Special field allows you to set any additional indent for the first line of a paragraph, or to set a hanging indent.

You should remember that all the indentations are relative to something else. As noted earlier, the left and right paragraph indents are relative to the page margins. Thus if you have a 1 inch right margin and you set a 3/4 inch right indent, then the paragraph will be printed so there is 1 3/4 inches of white space to the right of the paragraph. Likewise, a –1/2 inch right indent would result in only 1/2 inch of white space on the right.

The first-line indent is a bit different. It is always relative to the left indent for the paragraph. Thus, if you have a left margin of 1 inch, a left indent of 1 inch, and a first line indent of 1/2 inch, then the line will begin 2 1/2 inches from the left side of the paper. Subsequent lines will begin back at the left indent, 2 inches from the left side of the paper.

First-line indents are very handy; they eliminate the necessity of starting each paragraph by pressing the TAB key or entering five spaces (as my typing teacher always taught me). Hanging indents ("outdents") are used quite a bit in writing. These are the type of indents where the first line begins left of all the other lines in the paragraph. For instance, the following is considered a hanging indent:

- This paragraph uses a hanging indent. You will notice that the first line extends to the left of the regular paragraph indent to make room for the bullet and the space after, resulting in a look that is commonly used in computer and other technical books.

This type of indent is accomplished by setting the Special field to Hanging and then specifying how far you want the body of the paragraph indented. The first line remains set to the original left margin of the paragraph.

When you have finished changing how the paragraph should be indented, you can click on the OK button.

INDENTING WITH THE RULER

The ruler can be a big help in formatting. One of the things you can view and change on the ruler are the paragraph indents. Take a look at an example ruler:

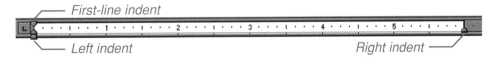

Notice the three triangles on the ruler. There are two at the left side and one at the right. Together, these three define the indents for the paragraph. The top triangle on the left side defines the first-line indent, while the bottom one defines the regular left indent. On the right, the triangle indicates the right indent.

You can change the indentation for the paragraph by using the mouse. Simply point to the triangle that represents the indent you want to change. Then press and hold down the left mouse button. As you move the mouse, the indent moves as well. When you release the mouse button, the indent remains at the new location, and the text in the paragraph is reformatted to reflect the new indents. If you want to move both the left and first-line indents, click and drag the box under the left indent triangle.

HOW PARAGRAPHS ARE PAGINATED

Earlier in this book you learned how Word for Windows handled pagination. It can either paginate your document automatically, or you can do it manually. As Word for Windows is deciding where page breaks should be inserted, it looks at where paragraphs occur. If you have a short paragraph (two or three lines) and the page break would normally occur in the middle of the paragraph, Word for Windows will not break it because it would mean leaving only a single line of the paragraph on a page. In typesetting, this is against the traditional rules. These lone lines are called *widows* or *orphans*. (The reasoning for this terminology is lost in the history of typesetting lore.) If the paragraph is longer, however, Word for Windows will go ahead and divide the paragraph between pages, placing at least two lines on either page.

Paginating in this way, for the most part, presents very little problem. There may be times, however, when you want to force a different type of pagination. Typically this is done for design purposes.

For example, you might want all the lines in a certain paragraph to never be split between pages, or you may want to make sure that Word for Windows always keeps a certain paragraph on the same page as another paragraph, for example, always keeping a figure caption with the figure. This type of pagination is easy to enforce. It is done by selecting Paragraph from the Format menu. When you do, select the Text Flow file card, and you will see the dialog box shown in Figure 15.2:

Pagination controls

Text Flow file card

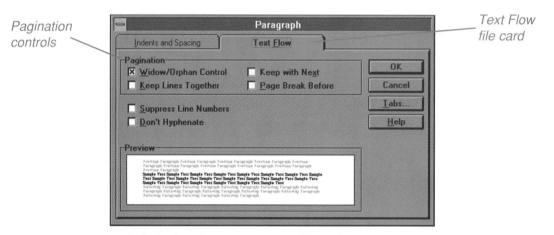

Figure 15.2 Paragraph dialog box showing Text Flow file card.

At the top of the dialog box is an area entitled *Pagination.* The four choices in this box allow you to indicate how you want the paragraph treated when Word for Windows is paginating your document. Each option can be selected by clicking on the check box to the left of the option. These options do the following:

Widow/Orphan Control allows you to determine whether Word for Windows will allow widows and orphans to exist at page breaks, as described earlier.

Keep Lines Together results in the entire paragraph being kept on one page. If you have long paragraphs, this option can result in some odd-looking pages, with large amounts of white space at the bottom of some pages.

Keep With Next is used to ensure that the current paragraph always appears on the same page as the paragraph that follows it. This, again, is often used for titles or heads within a document.

Page Break Before results in Word for Windows always starting this paragraph on a new page. You might want to use this option with certain types of titles or heads in your document.

When you have finished changing how the paragraph should affect pagination, you can click on the ░OK░ button.

PARAGRAPH SPACING

In typographical terms, the vertical spacing (space between lines) within a paragraph is referred to as *leading* (pronounced "ledd-ing"). This term originated in the early days of typesetting, when additional space was added between lines by adding thin strips of lead between the lines of type. Word for Windows allows you to control completely how much space there should be before, during, and after any paragraph.

When you choose the Paragraph option from the Format menu and choose the Indents and Spacing file card and you will see the Paragraph dialog box as shown in Figure 15.3:

Indents and Spacing
file card

Spacing
options

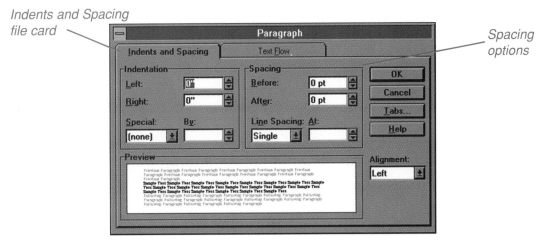

Figure 15.3 Paragraph dialog box showing Indents and Spacing file card.

The box in the center of the Paragraph dialog box contains three settings. The Before and After fields are where you can specify how much space should appear both before and after the paragraph. These measurements are usually given in points, but may be specified using any unit of measure you desire. The third field, Line Spacing, is the field that takes a bit more explanation. In Word for Windows, line spacing is the same as leading, which was described earlier. The setting in the Line Spacing field works in conjunction with the At field, allowing you to choose any line spacing desired.

In the box under Line Spacing, there are six choices you can make:

Single forces the paragraph to be single-spaced, with each line occupying the same as any other line. With this spacing you can get six lines per vertical inch of your document.

1.5 Lines tells each line of the paragraph to occupy 1 1/2 lines of space. Thus, you can get four lines per vertical inch of your document.

Double forces the paragraph to be double-spaced. If you choose this spacing for all paragraphs in your document, it will occupy twice as much space as a document formatted with single-spaced lines. With this spacing, every three lines represents another inch of your document.

At Least allows you to specify a minimum spacing you want to use. In operation, this type of spacing is similar to the Auto option, in that Word for Windows will adjust line spacing according to the largest font (or perhaps a graphic) on a line. However, it will not reduce spacing below whatever you specify in the At field.

Exactly allows you to specify an exact line spacing, for example 13.5 pt or .75 inch. This is for use when you want to make sure Word for Windows does not vary from an exact amount of space between lines.

Multiple is used if you want to choose a different leading than those listed above. For instance, you would use this option if you wanted leading set at three lines (triple-spaced text).

Once you have specified what line spacing you want to use, you can click on the `OK` button.

What You Need to Know

Paragraphs are the fundamental building blocks of a document. Word for Windows allows you quickly and easily to change how those paragraphs appear in relation to the rest of your document. Before leaving this lesson, make sure you understand how to do the following:

- ☑ Align a paragraph
- ☑ Indent a paragraph
- ☑ Change how a paragraph is paginated
- ☑ Change spacing before, after, and within a paragraph.

In the next lesson you will learn about another type of formatting that has an affect on your paragraphs—tabs.

Lesson 16

Changing and Setting Tabs

If you are familiar with typewriters, you are probably already familiar with tab stops. These are locations across a page to which your cursor will move when you press the TAB key. On a typewriter, pressing TAB simply moves the type element to the next tab stop. In Word for Windows, however, tab stops are much more powerful. You can set different types of tab stops that control how text is treated, and you can set different tab stops for each paragraph in your document. In this lesson you will learn about these tab stops, as well as the following:

- Setting default tab stops
- Setting tabs with the ribbon and ruler
- Setting tabs precisely

DIFFERENT TYPES OF TAB STOPS

In Word for Windows there are four different types of tabs—left, center, right, and decimal. Each of these defines how text is aligned to the tab stop when you press the TAB key. The first three types of tabs (left, center, and right) are similar in nature to paragraph alignment, as described in Lesson 15. For instance, when you set a left-aligned tab stop, the text after the tab stop is aligned so the tab is to the left of the text. A center tab stop results in text being centered on the tab, and a right-aligned tab is the opposite of a left-aligned one—all text is aligned so the tab is to the right of the text.

The final type of tab stop is used primarily when dealing with numbers. A decimal tab results in information being aligned so that the decimal point (or period) is aligned right at the tab stop. This helps keep columns of numbers neat and tidy.

DEFAULT TAB STOPS

There are two kinds of tabs—those that are implicitly set, and those that are explicitly set. For simplicity, implicit tabs are referred to as *default tabs,* while explicit tabs represent those that you set yourself (covered in the next two sections).

Default tabs are tabs that are assumed to be in place when you have not defined any other tabs. By default, Word for Windows uses default tab stops of 1/2 inch. When you press TAB, the cursor moves to the next default tab stop, 1/2 inch to the right. Since these are default tabs, they are not fancy; they are simply left-aligned tab stops.

You can change the default tab setting by choosing Tabs from the Format menu. You will then see the Tabs dialog box, as shown in Figure 16.1:

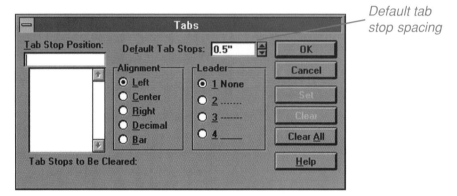

Figure 16.1 Tabs dialog box.

In the Default Tab Stops field at the top of the dialog box, specify a default spacing between tab stops. You can then click on the ⟨ OK ⟩ button, and the change will be made.

SETTING TABS WITH THE RULER

You can use the ruler to set your own tab stops, if desired. This is basically a two-step process, using the mouse:

1. Make sure the tab type, at the left side of the ruler, indicates the type of tab stop you want to set.

2. Click on the ruler where you want the tab stop located.

The tab type (mentioned in Step 1) can be any one of the tabs shown in Table 16.1:

Button	Meaning
L	Left-aligned tab
⊥	Center-aligned tab
⅃	Right-aligned tab
⊥	Decimal-aligned tab

Table 16.1 *The four tab indicators in Word for Windows.*

To select one of the tab types, simply click on the marker that is displayed. Word for Windows will cycle through all four tab types.

These indicators are also the same markers that will appear on the ruler. As an example of how to do this, let's suppose you want to set a center-aligned tab at 2 inches from my left margin. First, click the ⊥ button, and then use the mouse to click at this location on the ruler. The tab is then inserted at that location and indicated on the ruler:

Center-aligned tab stop

One other interesting technique you can use is to move tabs along the ruler. If you have already placed a tab and you decide you want it moved elsewhere, all you need to do is point to the tab stop on the ruler and press and drag the tab marker (hold down the left mouse button—as you move the mouse, the tab stop moves as well). When you release the mouse button, the tab is set at the new location.

If you later want to delete a tab, you can point to it with the mouse cursor, press and hold down the left mouse button, and drag the tab off the ruler. When you do, it is deleted from the paragraph.

SETTING TABS PRECISELY

While you can set and change tabs by using the ribbon and the ruler, you cannot control them precisely. For instance, if you needed a tab exactly at 2.875 inches from the left margin, you would be lucky if you could precisely judge that location using the ruler. In these instances, you will want to use the Tabs option from the Format menu. Word for Windows displays the Tabs dialog box, as shown in Figure 16.2:

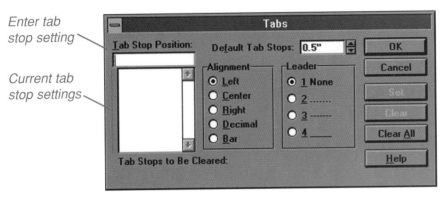

Enter tab stop setting

Current tab stop settings

Figure 16.2 Tabs dialog box.

At the left of the dialog box is a list of currently set tab stops. Notice that the default tab stops are not listed here—only those that have been explicitly set. In the Tab Stop Position field at the top of the list you can enter a measurement for the tab stop. Then you only need to choose an Alignment type, choose a leader, and click on **Set**.

A *leader* is the character that should appear in place of the actual tab character. Dots (periods) called *ellipses* are often used as a tab leader so the reader's eye can easily follow from the end of a text line to the number associated with that line. This typographical device is often employed in a Table of Contents. Word for Windows allows you to specify three different types of leaders (four, if you count None as a leader type).

You can continue to set tab stops, or you can select existing tab stops and click on **Clear** to remove them. When you have finished setting tabs, click on the **OK** button.

WHAT YOU NEED TO KNOW

Tab stops have many uses in a document. They are used to align text within a line, and can greatly increase the readability of many types of material. Word for Windows allows you to set tab stops for individual paragraphs within your document. Before moving on to character formatting, you should take a moment to make sure you understand the following:

- ☑ There are four different types of tabs within Word for Windows.
- ☑ Word for Windows uses default tab stops if none have been explicitly set.
- ☑ Leaders are characters used in place of a tab character on a printout.

In addition, you should know how to

- ☑ Change the default tab stop setting
- ☑ Set tabs using the ribbon and ruler
- ☑ Change and delete tab stops using the ribbon and ruler
- ☑ Set and clear tab stops using the Tabs option from the Format menu
- ☑ Set a leader character for a tab stop

If you are fuzzy on any of these items, you should take a moment to review the material in this lesson, since tabs are such a common tool in documents. You will want to be comfortable with tabs before proceeding.

Lesson 17

Changing How Characters Look

Formatting individual characters is what most people think of when you mention formatting. Perhaps this is because you can spend the largest amount of time formatting the characters in your document. However, as you have learned in previous lessons, character formatting is not the only type of formatting you can do in Word for Windows. And as you will learn in this lesson, character formatting is relatively easy and can have a great impact on the overall appearance of your document.

In this lesson you will be learning the following:

- What a font is

- How you can apply fonts to your text

- How you can change text attributes

- How you can change point sizes

WHAT IS A FONT?

The terms *font* and *typeface* are often used interchangeably. In simple terms, they represent a certain way of printing letters, numbers, and other symbols. These fonts are given names that are either dictated by tradition or loosely represent the appearance of the font. For instance, Courier is a common font, as are Helvetica and Times Roman. There are literally thousands of fonts on the market today, each being sold by different vendors. Word for Windows supports any font that you can install into Windows, including bitmap, Adobe, and TrueType fonts.

Fonts are measured in *points*. A point is roughly equivalent to 1/72 of an inch. Thus, a 10-point typeface has characters that are roughly 10/72 of an inch in height. Later in this lesson you will learn how to change the height of a font within Word for Windows; all such changes are done using points.

In general, there are four types of fonts. These are:

- Serif fonts

- Sans serif fonts

- Symbol fonts

- Decorative fonts

Serif fonts are those that have embellishments (*serifs*) on the letters that make them appear more pleasing and less angular. For example, the font used in this book is a serif font. Notice the serifs on the following New Century Schoolbook type sample:

Serifs ——————This has serifs

A sans serif font (meaning, literally, *without serif*) does not have the flourishes on the strokes of each letter. For instance, the following is in Helvetica, a common sans serif font:

This has no serifs

While sans serif is fine for shorter lines of text and headlines, a serif font is better suited for longer lines and text that will probably be read for longer periods of time.

Symbol fonts are used to add graphics symbols to a document. Word for Windows supports many different types of symbol fonts such as Symbol, Wingdings, and Zapf Dingbats. These fonts may include characters such as the following:

❄〰✶✦ ♋■□♏♌♓↗

Finally, decorative fonts are used primarily for titles and headings. They are not good for general text, as they are typically large, bold, and designed to stand out from other typefaces around them. Examples include Cooper, Billboard, Ink Pad, Cargo, or Zapf Chancery. The following is an example using the Zapf Chancery typeface:

This is decorative

CHANGING TYPEFACES

If you want to change a typeface within Word for Windows, you must first select the text you want to format. This is done as was described in Lesson 8, "Entering and Changing Text." Once the text is selected, you can change the typeface by clicking on the arrow next to the typeface field on the Formatting toolbar. When you do, you will see a list of typefaces from which you can choose:

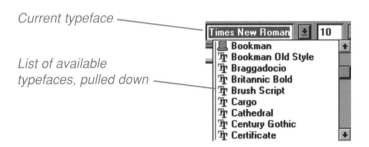

Current typeface

List of available typefaces, pulled down

You can scroll through the available typefaces the same way you scroll through many other options within Word for Windows. When you select a typeface, the change is made immediately.

APPLYING TEXT ATTRIBUTES

Text attributes can be viewed as nothing more than modifications to the base font. For instance, you might use the bold attribute to emphasize your text, or italics might be used to indicate a quote. Common text attributes can be easily applied using the buttons on the Formatting toolbar. Table 17.1 shows the three text attribute buttons provided:

Button	Meaning
B	Bold
I	Italics
U	Underlined

Table 17.1 The character attribute buttons on the Formatting toolbar.

There are other attributes, such as strikethrough, hidden, small caps, and all caps, but these attributes cannot be applied using the Formatting toolbar. Instead, you must use the full character formatting features of Word for Windows. This is done by using the menus, as described later in this lesson.

Changing Point Sizes

Earlier in this lesson you learned that type sizes are specified in points. This is a typographer's measure that is equal to approximately 1/72 of an inch. To change the point size of a text selection, you can use the Formatting toolbar. Just to the left of the text attribute buttons is the point size field. If you click on the arrow to the right of this field, you are presented with a list of point sizes you can choose:

Current point size

List of common point sizes, pulled down

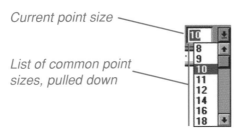

Word for Windows allows you to specify any font size between 1 and 1638 points. (This depends, of course, on the capabilities of your printer.) To pick a point size, simply scroll through the list and choose the one you want. Click on the point size, and your text is updated.

Note: You can also type a point size into the field in place of the highlighted current point size if you want to change your text to a size that is not on the list.

As it stores your document on disk, Word for Windows keeps track of point sizes (along with other text formatting information). You can, if you desire, change the point size (as well as text attribute and font) of every letter in your document. While such a creation might be difficult to read, it is certainly not beyond the capabilities of Word for Windows.

Changing Character Format All At Once

So far in this lesson you have learned how to modify character formatting using the Formatting toolbar. While there are many tasks you can perform with the Formatting toolbar, there are some that are best left to the Font option from the Format menu. When you choose this option, you will see the Font dialog box, as shown in Figure 17.1. Make sure you have the Font file card selected.

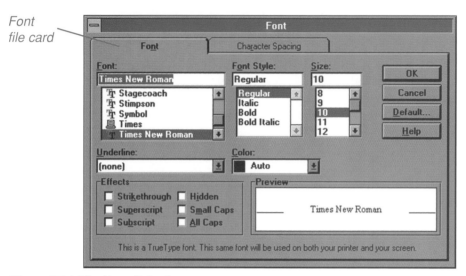

Font file card

Figure 17.1 *The Font dialog box.*

Based on earlier discussions, many of the fields in this dialog box should already look familiar. One thing you should notice right away, however, is that there are quite a few more attributes you can apply to your text. These are all contained within the Effects box at the lower-left corner of the dialog box.

Word for Windows also allows you to change the color of your text. This is done by clicking on the arrow to the right of the Color field. Click on this to see samples of colors you can apply to your text. If you don't have a color printer, don't worry—you can still use the color to highlight text on the screen, and Word for Windows will print the text in black and white, as if the colors had not been changed at all.

If you want to underline your text, you have choices about the type of underline, which you can make in the Underline field.

As you make any changes to the character formatting, you can see the effect in the sample text shown in the dialog box. This sample text is the font name, or if you have made a text selection, it is the first part of the text you selected. When you are satisfied with the formatting you have applied, click on the OK button.

A WORD ABOUT RESPONSIBLE FORMATTING

Word for Windows provides quite a wide assortment of character formatting options. You can virtually make your text look any way you desire. As you add more and more fonts, your options increase just that much more. All these options and capabilities might lead you to think you absolutely must use them. Before you succumb to this temptation, take a moment to reflect on what you consider pleasant reading. Chances are it is something that is simple and to the point.

If you add too many fonts and change sizes or attributes too often, your desired effect will be lost, leaving confusion in its wake. It is not the place of this book to provide design information, but you should realize that when working with type, simpler is generally better. If you are interested in this area, or if you find yourself doing quite a bit of design work using type, you should invest in one or more specialized desktop publishing books. While Word for Windows is not a full-blown desktop publishing program, many of the guidelines applicable for those programs are also applicable for Word for Windows.

WHAT YOU NEED TO KNOW

Character formatting is the most often used type of formatting offered by Word for Windows. It is not unusual to spend only a few minutes entering your text and then another couple of hours formatting it to get it just right.

In this lesson you have learned the following information, all of which you can use in formatting your documents:

☑ What a font is

☑ How fonts differ from each other

☑ How to change fonts

☑ How to change text attributes

☑ How to change point sizes

☑ How to change character formatting on the Formatting toolbar

☑ How to change character formatting using the Format menu

☑ How to format characters sensibly

Once you have mastered character formatting, you know all there is to know about the basics of Word for Windows formatting. In the next lesson you will learn how you can combine some of these formatting skills to develop different types of lists.

Lesson 18

Working with Lists

Lists are used extensively in many types of documents. In this lesson you will learn:

- How to create a bulleted list

- How to control the type of bullets used

- How to create a numbered list

- How to change the number format used

- How to change between list types

CREATING A BULLETED LIST

A *bulleted list* is a group of items that begin with a special symbol called a *bullet.* This is a typographical term denoting a special character used to mark the start of the item in the list. In most instances, a bullet is a small dot, as in the bulleted list used to begin this lesson. However, the bullet can be any of a number of different symbols, as you shall learn in the next section. You use a bulleted list when the items in the list need not necessarily be in a sequential order.

When there are multiple lines in any given list item, the extra lines are indented so they begin at the same point as the first line. For instance, the following is an item in a bulleted list that contains more than one line:

- This is an item in the bulleted list. Notice that the item employs what is called a *hanging indent,* meaning that the first line begins at the left margin, but all subsequent lines are indented.

The easiest way to create a bulleted list is to select the paragraphs you want included in the list, and then use the ▦ tool. Word for Windows takes care of adding the bullet and adjusting the margins and indent.

CHANGING BULLET TYPES

Bullets used by Word for Windows do not have to be just dots. They can be any character you designate. The manner in which Word for Windows creates bulleted lists is controlled by selecting the Bullets and Numbering option from the Format menu. Make sure you select the Bulleted file card. When you do, you will see a dialog box similar to Figure 18.1:

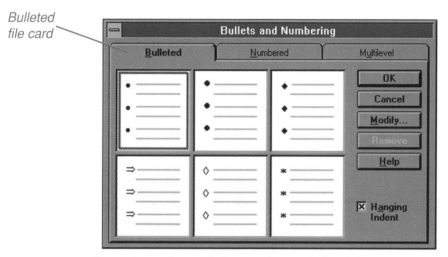

Bulleted file card

Figure 18.1 Bullets and Numbering dialog box showing bulleted file card.

Notice that there are six predefined bullet types. You can change any of these, however, by simply clicking on the Modify... button. When you do, you will be able to modify the bullets used by Word for Windows in any way desired.

CREATING A NUMBERED LIST

A *numbered list* is closely related to a bulleted list, except that sequential numbers are used to denote items in the list. These types of lists are typically used when you need to develop a series of steps you want the reader to follow in order, as shown here:

1. First, you do this.
2. Then you perform this step.
3. Followed by this step.
4. Finally, you do the last step.

A numbered list is created by highlighting the paragraphs you want included in the list, and then clicking on the ▤ tool. Word for Windows takes care of adding the number, the tab, and any hanging indents.

CHANGING NUMBER FORMAT

Just as Word for Windows allows you to change the type of bullets used, you can also change the type of numbers used. This is done by selecting the Bullets and Numbering option from the Format menu. Make sure the Numbered file card is selected at the top of the dialog box. You will then see a dialog box similar to Figure 18.2:

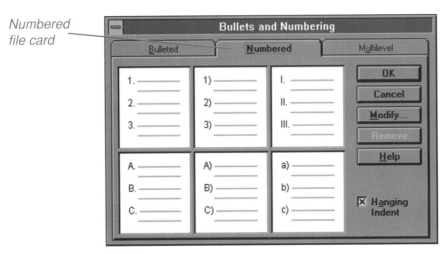

Figure 18.2 Bullets and Numbering dialog box showing Numbered file card.

Choose a predefined list format, or click on Modify... to change the appearance of one of the list presets. You can change the text before the number, the type of number, the text after the number, and the font used for the numbers.

WHAT YOU NEED TO KNOW

Word for Windows allows you to define lists quickly and easily. There are two types of lists you can create, and you should be familiar with these:

Bulleted lists are preceded by individual symbols called bullets. You can see that we've used a bullet other than a dot here.

Numbered lists are preceded by numbers.

Lesson 19

Adding Headers and Footers

Headers and *footers* appear at the top and bottom of each page in your document. For instance, each page in this book has a header at the top, which consists of the book name or the lesson name. These headers are sometimes called *running heads.* At the bottom of each page in the book is a footer, which consists of the page number.

Word for Windows allows you to define quickly and easily how you want page headers and footers to appear. In this lesson you will learn:

- How to add headers and footers to your document
- How to add special characters to your headers and footers
- How to change headers and footers for different page types

ADDING HEADERS AND FOOTERS

When you first create a document, Word for Windows does not print headers or footers. This is not because they aren't there (they really are), but because you have not defined them. To do this, you choose the Header and Footer option from the View menu. When you do, Word for Windows changes to Page Layout viewing mode, highlights the header area, and displays the Header and Footer toolbar, as shown in Figure 19.1:

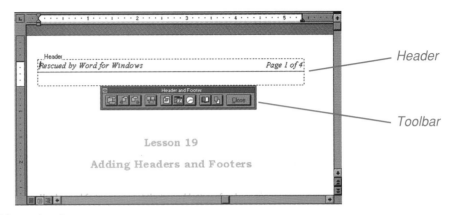

Figure 19.1 Adding a header.

Whatever you type in this Header area will appear as the header in your document. You can even include multiple lines, if desired. When you have finished defining the header (or footer), you can select the [Close] button. The window is removed, and you are returned to your original viewing mode, but the header has been defined and will print on each page of your document.

Word for Windows allows you to add special characters to your header or footer, and to perform special functions, as well. An example of special characters is the page number, the current time, or the current date. These are easily added by using the buttons on the Header and Footer toolbar. There are ten buttons in this window, which are described in Table 19.1:

Button	Function
	Jumps to the header or the footer (depending on which you are currently working on)
	Displays the header and footer for the previous section
	Displays the header and footer for the following section
	Links or unlinks this header and footer to the one in the previous section
	Adds the current page number
	Adds the current date
	Adds the current time
	Shows the Page Setup dialog box
	Changes the main text viewing mode.
Close	Closes the Header and Footer toolbar and returns to the original viewing mode

Table 19.1 The buttons on the Header and Footer toolbar.

CONTROLLING PAGES

Word for Windows allows you to control the types of headers and footers in your document. This is done by either selecting Page Setup from the File menu or by clicking on the tool on the Header and Footer toolbar. You will then see the Page Setup dialog box, as shown in Figure 19.2; make sure the Layout file card is selected:

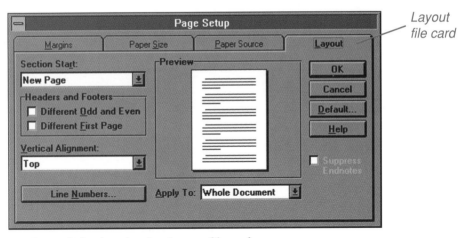

Figure 19.2 Page Setup dialog box showing Layout file card.

There are two check boxes on the dialog box that allow you to control the type of headers and footers you define. If you click on the Different Odd and Even check box, then you can define different headers and footers for both odd and even pages in your document. If you select the Different First Page check box, then Word for Windows assumes you want to define a different header and footer for the first page of your document. To change the header or footer for one of these pages, simply go to that page (for instance, the first page or an odd or even page) and make your changes. Word for Windows takes care of ensuring that the proper header or footer is printed on the appropriate page.

WHAT YOU NEED TO KNOW

Headers and footers can add a professional touch to your documents. Word for Windows allows you to define quickly and easily how you want your headers and footers to appear. In this lesson you should have learned the following:

☑ How to add headers and footers to your document

☑ How to display and hide the Header and Footer window

☑ How to insert special characters into a header or footer

☑ How to define headers and footers for different types of pages

USING TEMPLATES AND STYLES

Section Four

Templates are nothing more than a pattern for how you want your documents to look. Styles, which can be a part of your templates, allow you to define how you want different characters and paragraphs within your document to look. By using templates (including those supplied with Word for Windows), you can save both time and effort. Styles, on the other hand, allow you to format entire paragraphs to look a specific way quickly. This section teaches you how you can use both templates and styles to maximize your productivity and quickly standardize the appearance of your documents.

Lesson 20

What Are Templates?

A *template* is a pattern you can use for your documents. Through the effective use of templates, you can ensure that similar documents use the same formatting and have the same general appearance.

This lesson lays the groundwork you will need in order to understand and use both templates and styles. In this lesson you will learn:

- How to create a template
- How to use template files
- How templates are updated
- What happens when you change templates

CREATING A TEMPLATE

Templates are nothing but specialized document files. This means you can define a document as you normally would and then save it as a template file. When you later load the template, all the information in the original file is used as the template, or pattern, for the new document you are creating.

Effective use of templates, however, requires that you give some careful thought to what you want in your template. They can contain any of the following:

- Formatting styles (as covered in Lesson 21)
- Macros (as covered in Lesson 42)
- *Boilerplate* text (which remains the same while individual document parts, such as the name of the recipient, change), including headers and footers

In addition, any changes you may make to the menus or toolbar are stored with the template file. Thus, using a template file eliminates the need to "re-create the wheel" every time you want to create a new document that is similar to one you have already done.

To create a template file, first set up a document the way you want it. Make sure you have defined all the styles for the document, as well as any macros you might need. Then delete the text that will change from document to document. Finally, choose the Save As command from the File menu to see a dialog box similar to Figure 20.1:

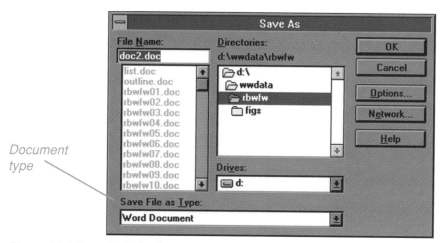

Figure 20.1 Save As dialog box.

In the Save File as Type field at the bottom of the dialog box, make sure you select Document Template. The file then receives a special DOT extension. This file should be saved wherever other DOT files are saved in your system. Typically this is the WINWORD directory, but it may have been changed to a different directory. If you are in doubt as to where the templates are stored, use the File Manager to search for files with the DOT extension. (For information on how to do this, refer to the book *Rescued by Windows,* Jamsa Press, 1993.)

Once saved, the template is available for use by other documents.

USING A TEMPLATE AGAIN

To use a template again, simply specify it when you create a new document. For instance, let's assume you named your template RESCBY.DOT. You could later use the New command from the File menu to specify this as the template file you want to use. When you choose the command, you will see a dialog box similar to Figure 20.2:

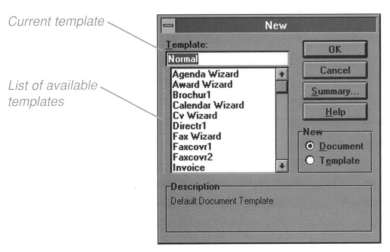

Current template

List of available templates

Figure 20.2 New dialog box.

The Template list allows you to indicate which template you want to use with this document. By default, Word for Windows uses the NORMAL template. You can specify any other template you desire, however. In this case, you should select the RESCBY template, and then click on [OK]. This action makes all the defaults you defined within RESCBY a part of the new document.

UPDATING A TEMPLATE

The easiest way to update a template is to simply load it again, as you would any other document, and make changes. When you save your changes, they are available for any other documents you may create based on the template.

CHANGING TEMPLATES

To change the template attached to a document, you first select the Templates option from the File menu. You will then see the Templates and Add-Ins dialog box, as shown in Figure 20.3:

Currently
attached
template

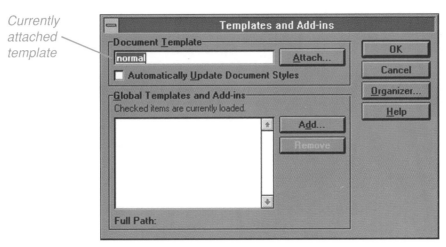

Figure 20.3 *Templates and Add-Ins dialog box.*

Next, click on the Attach... button. The Attach Template dialog box will appear, as shown in Figure 20.4, where you can see a list of the available templates and select the template you want to use:

List of
available
templates

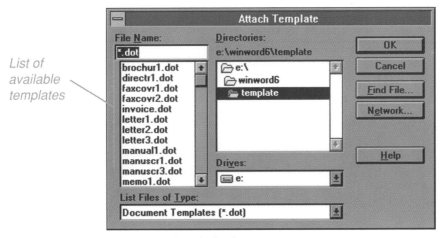

Figure 20.4 *The Attach Template dialog box.*

Then you click on the `OK` button to make the change complete.

Remember that templates are, by their nature, a starting point for a document. When you change templates for an existing document, you have already passed the starting point, however. The only thing used from the new template is the menu and toolbar definitions. The styles and boilerplate text are ignored; they are only used if you are creating a new document using the template. Later in this section, in Lesson 23, you will learn how to update style information.

WHAT YOU NEED TO KNOW

Templates allow you to define quickly and easily how a document should appear. Word for Windows makes it easy to create templates—all you need to do is store a regular document as a template file. In this lesson you have learned how to do the following:

- ☑ Create a template
- ☑ Use template files
- ☑ Change and update templates
- ☑ Change the template attached to a document

Lesson 21

Understanding Styles

In the previous lesson you learned how templates are patterns you can use to define how you want a document to look. In this lesson you will learn about another type of pattern you can define—styles. Styles allow you to define how you want individual paragraphs and characters to look within your document. Specifically, this lesson will teach you:

- How to create styles
- How to make changes to existing styles
- How to save styles

CREATING STYLES

As already mentioned, a style is nothing more than a pattern for how you want a paragraph or selected characters to look. For example, if you wanted a heading of a type that appears frequently throughout your document to be in 15-point Garamond font, boldface, italic, blue, and in small caps, with two line spaces above it and 1 1/2 line spaces below, you could perform each of these formatting tasks, one by one, each time you type such a head, or you could define a style (perhaps named Heading 1) that performs all of these formatting tasks with the click of a button. To define a style, you choose the Style option from the Format menu, then click on the **New...** button. You will see the New Style dialog box on your screen, as shown in Figure 21.1:

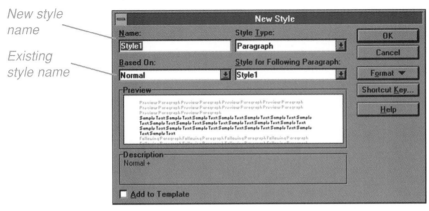

Figure 21.1 The New Style dialog box.

In the Name field at the top of the dialog box, you can indicate the name of the style you want to define.

The simplest way to define a style is to base it on an existing style. Word for Windows allows you to do this by changing the value in the Based On field. If you change this to an existing style, Word for Windows will base all the attributes of the new style on the existing one. You can then make changes to this "starting point."

In the Style Type field you can specify whether you are creating a paragraph style or a character style. You should make your choice based on whether you want this style to be used for formatting paragraphs or characters.

Click on the [Format ▼] button to see a list of characteristics you can change for this style. Each of these options displays a formatting dialog box, with which you are probably familiar. These formatting options were covered in the previous section of this book.

Finally, notice that the dialog box contains a field called Style for Following Paragraph. By selecting a style in this field, you define how you want Word for Windows to behave when you are entering text and you press ENTER. For instance, let's assume you have defined two styles in your document. The first is named RegStyle, and the second is BoldStyle. Further, let's assume that you set the Next Style field for BoldStyle to be RegStyle. Now, if you are entering text using the BoldStyle style, and you press ENTER, Word for Windows automatically switches the format of the next paragraph to RegStyle. If used effectively, this is an extremely powerful feature.

When you are satisfied with how you have defined your new style, you can click on the [OK] button.

CHANGING EXISTING STYLES

Styles within Word for Windows can be easily changed at any time. This is done by choosing the Style option from the Format menu. You will then see the New Styles dialog box, presented earlier in this lesson. To change an existing style:

1. Select, within the Styles list, the style you want to change.

2. Click on [Modify...].

3. Make the formatting changes as desired.

4. Click on the [OK] button.

SAVING STYLES

There is very little you need to do to save styles. In fact, there are only two requirements. The first is to make sure you click on the [OK] button instead of the [Cancel] button in the Style dialog box. The second is to simply save your document. Styles are automatically saved with the document on which you are working.

WHAT YOU NEED TO KNOW

The information presented in this lesson is absolutely critical to working through the next three lessons. At this point you should understand the following thoroughly:

- ☑ How to add a style
- ☑ How to display default style names
- ☑ How to change an existing style
- ☑ How to save styles

If you are fuzzy on any of these concepts, make sure you review this lesson thoroughly.

Lesson 22

Using Styles in Your Document

In Lesson 21 you learned basic information about styles, as well as how to define and change them. In this lesson you will start to apply styles to your document. In this lesson you will learn

- How to display style information
- How to apply styles
- The advantages of using styles
- How to apply default paragraph formats
- How to apply default character formats

DISPLAYING STYLE INFORMATION

As you begin to work with styles, you will find it helpful to know which styles you are using within your document. While the name of the style for the paragraph that your cursor is in is displayed on the box at the left of the Formatting toolbar, this is best done by displaying the *style area*, an area to the left of each paragraph that shows the name of the style attached to it. Normally the style area is not displayed; however you can instruct Word for Windows to display it to the left of your document. This is done by selecting Options from the Tools menu. Since you have not used this dialog box in the past several lessons, make sure that the View file card is selected, as shown in Figure 22.1:

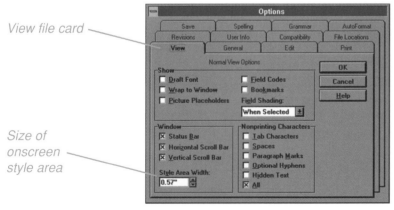

Figure 22.1 Options dialog box showing View file card.

At the lower-left corner of the dialog box is a field called Style Area Width. By default, this width is set to 0, meaning the style area is not displayed. Set this to a value around 0.5 to 0.8 inches. When you click on the OK button, your Word for Windows document window changes to be similar to the one shown in Figure 22.2:

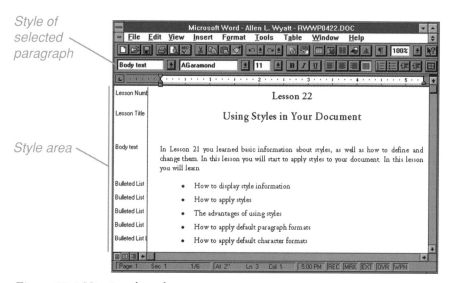

Figure 22.2 Viewing the style area.

The area at the left of the document is the style area. It shows the style name assigned to each paragraph in your document. In this way you can determine if the paragraph formatting has been done correctly for each paragraph.

APPLYING STYLES

There are two ways you can apply styles in your document. The first (and easiest) is to use the Formatting toolbar. The other method is to use the menus.

At the left side of the Formatting toolbar is a field that indicates the style of the paragraph in which the cursor is positioned. If you have selected more than one paragraph, and all the paragraphs are formatted the same, the field will still display the style name. If, however, different paragraphs within your selection are formatted using different styles, then the field will be blank.

To apply a style with the Formatting toolbar, simply click on the arrow at the right of the style name field. Paragraph styles are listed in bold type, while character styles are listed in regular type. You can then pick a style from the list of defined styles. The attributes you defined for that style are then applied to the text in the selected paragraphs.

The other method of applying styles is to use the menus. First, make sure the cursor is positioned in the paragraph you want to format, that you have selected a group of paragraphs to format, or that you have selected the text you want to format. Then select Style from the Format menu. You will see the Style dialog box, as shown in Figure 22.3:

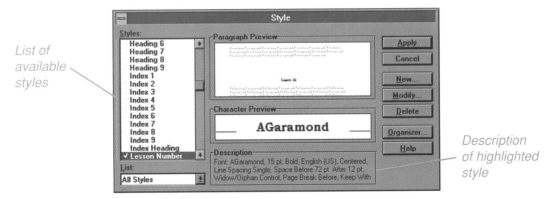

List of available styles

Description of highlighted style

Figure 22.3 Style dialog box.

In the Styles list, select the style you want to use. Then click on the [Apply] button. The attributes for that style are then applied to the selected text.

Note: You can also bring up the Style dialog box by pressing CTRL-SHIFT-S *twice.*

ADVANTAGES OF STYLES

The largest single advantage of styles is that you only have to define a format once, and then it can be applied throughout your document. For instance, if you are using the predefined style called Normal, and you later decide that you want these types of paragraphs to be indented by 1/2 inch, then all you need to do is change the style. After changing the style, every paragraph in your document that is formatted with the Normal style will be indented 1/2 inch. This is done automatically; there is nothing else that needs to be done on your part.

DEFAULT PARAGRAPH FORMATTING

In any Word for Windows document, there is one default paragraph format. The style name for this format is Normal, and there are two ways you can apply it. The first is to simply use the techniques discussed in the previous lesson (using the formatting toolbar or the menus). The second method is to use CTRL-SHIFT-N, which applies the Normal style to the paragraph where the insertion point is located.

In addition to setting paragraph formatting back to the Normal style, you might also want to remove any additional paragraph formatting you have applied. For instance, if you formatted a paragraph as Heading 1 and then manually changed the paragraph alignment for that paragraph, you might want to set it back to the default settings as defined for the Heading 1 style. This is done by using CTRL-Q, which sets the paragraph attributes (indents, tabs, alignment, and so on) back to their defaults for the paragraph style applied to the paragraph.

DEFAULT CHARACTER FORMATS

There may be times when you apply a paragraph style, and the characters within the paragraph do not look like you believe they should in this paragraph style. It is very possible to apply a style to a paragraph and not have the characters within the paragraph change to what they are supposed to be. While this may sound confusing, it makes perfect sense if you had specifically applied a character attribute or style to the text within the paragraph. When you do this, Word for Windows assumes you have a purpose for doing it, and it won't change it unless you tell it to.

To change character formatting to the default for the given paragraph style, simply select the entire paragraph and press CTRL-SPACEBAR. This removes all character attributes such as bold, italics, small caps, strikethrough, and so on, and sets the characters back to whatever format is defined for that paragraph style.

Note: Remember, if the characters within a paragraph do not look right—they do not look like you think they should for the type of paragraph style you are using—you should highlight the paragraph and press CTRL-SPACEBAR.

WHAT YOU NEED TO KNOW

Styles are a powerful feature of Word for Windows. They allow you to apply a consistent, professional look to your documents with a minimum of effort. In this lesson you have learned the following about styles:

- ☑ How to display the style area
- ☑ How to apply styles
- ☑ The major benefit of working with styles
- ☑ How to set paragraphs to the predefined Normal style
- ☑ How to remove paragraph formatting
- ☑ How to return character formatting to the default for the paragraph style

In the next lesson you will learn how you can remove any formatting you have applied to your text.

Lesson 23

Updating Your Template

You began this section in Lesson 20 by learning what templates are and how they can be used in Word for Windows. In this lesson you revisit templates to finish out the section and learn the following:

- How templates can be updated
- How you can automatically update styles from a template
- How you can copy styles between templates manually

These skills will help you complete your knowledge of how styles and templates work together. By applying this knowledge on a daily basis, you can learn to use both styles and templates to increase your productivity and make your documents more professional looking.

UPDATING TEMPLATES

In Lesson 20 you learned a bit about how you can make changes to an existing template. Loading and physically changing the template file is not the only way to make changes, however. Word for Windows also allows you to quickly make changes to the styles in a template. Doing this is a two-step process.

First, you must make sure the template you want to change is attached to your document. This was already covered in Lesson 20. Second, you tell Word for Windows to update the template. This is done when you are changing styles, as described in Lesson 21. You will remember that you change styles by selecting Style from the Format menu and clicking on the Modify... button. You see the Modify Style dialog box, as in Figure 23.1:

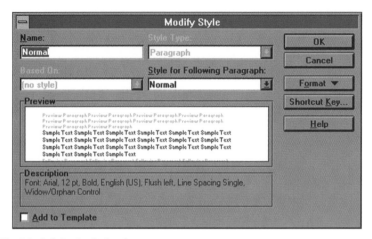

Figure 23.1 *The Modify Style dialog box.*

Notice the Add to Template check box in the lower-left corner of the dialog box. If you select this check box, Word for Windows will add any style changes to the template.

Note: There is one important caveat to remember here. Word for Windows will not actually update the template until you close or save the current document file. If you do not do either of these (for instance, if you just turn the power off), then the template is not updated with your changes.

UPDATING STYLES

You have already learned that templates do nothing but provide a starting point for a document. After that, all style information is stored with the document. If you make any style changes to the original template, they are not automatically reflected in any document to which that template may be attached. This is not entirely true, however. Word for Windows does provide two ways you can update styles in a document template—automatically and manually.

AUTOMATIC STYLE UPDATING

If you are familiar with Word for DOS, you already know that it handles style sheets (a form of a template limited to styles) differently than Word for Windows handles templates. In Word for DOS, whenever you make a change to a style sheet, the change is automatically reflected in every document that uses that style sheet.

Before version 6.0, this was not the case with Word for Windows. Now, however, you can tell Word for Windows to automatically update the current document every time there is a change to the template. This is done by selecting the Templates option from the File menu. When you do, you will see the Templates and Add-ins dialog box, as shown in Figure 23.2:

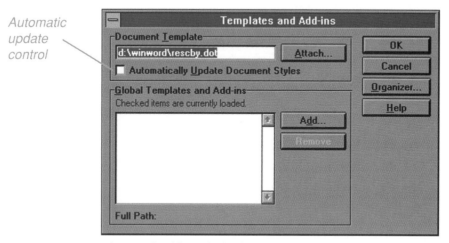

Figure 23.2 *Templates and Add-ins dialog box.*

Notice, right under the Document Template name, there is a check box labeled Automatically Update Document Styles. If you select this check box, then every time there is a change in the styles in the template, the change is reflected in the current document. This is consistent with how styles were treated in older versions of Word (the ones for DOS). If you do not enable automatic updating, then Word for Windows behaves as in earlier Windows versions—styles are not updated unless you do it automatically.

When you have finished making your changes in this dialog box, click on ▐ OK ▌.

MANUAL STYLE UPDATING

Word for Windows allows you great control over moving information between documents and templates. This is accomplished by using the template organizer, a new feature of Word for Windows 6.0. The easiest way to access this feature is to choose the Style option from the Format menu and then click on the ▐ Organizer... ▌ button. Make sure the Styles file card is selected; when you do, the Organizer dialog box will appear like Figure 23.3:

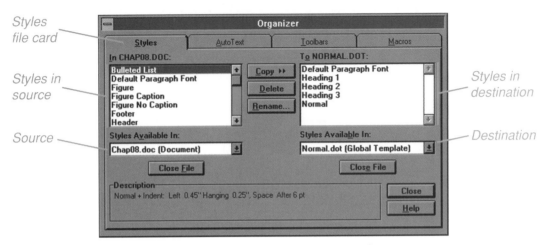

Figure 23.3 The Organizer Dialog box, with Styles file card selected.

On the left side of this dialog box you can specify the source file or template for the styles you wish to copy. On the right side, you choose the destination. The buttons between the two style lists (source and destination) allow you to control the copying, deletion, or renaming of styles.

Once you have organized your styles as desired, you can exit the Organizer dialog box by clicking on the [Close] button. If you made changes to the template stored with the current document, those changes are reflected immediately.

WHAT YOU NEED TO KNOW

Templates and styles complement each other and allow you to define patterns you want to use for both your documents and for text within your documents. Using the techniques described in this lesson, you can

- ☑ Update the styles in your template file as you change them
- ☑ Enable automatic updating of styles from a template
- ☑ Organize styles between any Word for Windows files manually

USING SOME TOOLS

Section Five

Word for Windows includes many tools to make you more productive. These tools include a spelling checker, a thesaurus, and a grammar checker. Not only can the spelling checker provide correct spellings, but it can also allow you to create specialized dictionaries to reflect your type of writing. The thesaurus can be used to uncover synonyms and antonyms that will enrich your prose. The grammar checker uses standard grammar rules to suggest changes to improve your writing style. By the end of this section you will learn how these three tools can help you improve the quality of your writing.

Lesson 24

Finding Alternative Words

Have you ever been in a situation where you didn't have quite the right word to describe your thoughts? Perhaps you knew a word that was close, but the exact word you were looking for escaped you. If you can identify with this situation, then you will appreciate one of the most overlooked tools in Word for Windows, the thesaurus. By the time you finish this lesson, you will know how to

- Look up a synonym

- Look up an antonym

- Look up additional words

- Replace a word with one of these

Word for Windows provides a complete thesaurus, which you can use to find words to enrich your writing.

LOOKING UP A SYNONYM

The first step in looking up a synonym for a word is to position the cursor on the word. You can then start the thesaurus in either of two ways. The first method is by pressing SHIFT-F7, and the second is to choose Thesaurus from the Tools menu.

For instance, let's assume you want to find a synonym for the word *method*. First, position the cursor anywhere within the word; then use one of the two methods to access the thesaurus. When you do, you will see the Thesaurus dialog box, as in Figure 24.1:

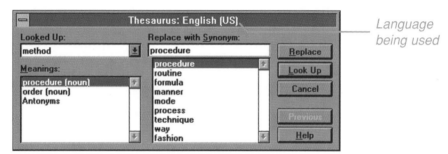

Figure 24.1 The Thesaurus dialog box.

At the top, the thesaurus being used is the default, English (US), or the language that you, or the author, have selected with the Language option of the Tools menu. On the left side of the dialog box is a list of meanings for the word. This list of meanings is necessary because many words can have multiple meanings, depending on how they are used. For instance, in one context a word might be used as a noun, while in another it is a verb. You should select the meaning that is closest to your intended meaning. The synonym list on the right side of the dialog box will then reflect different synonyms for the word.

To select a word, use the mouse to click on a word in the synonym list. This word then appears in the Replace With Synonym field at the top of the dialog box. When you click on the `Replace` button, the selected word replaces the original word in your document.

LOOKING UP ANTONYMS AND RELATED WORDS

For some words, Word for Windows may include *antonyms* or related words. An antonym is the opposite of the selected word. If there are antonyms available for a word, the word *Antonyms* will appear in the Meanings list. If related words are available, the term *Related words* will appear. When you select either of these, the synonym list on the right changes to an antonym or related word list. You can then select words from this list in the same way in which you selected synonyms.

LOOKING UP ADDITIONAL WORDS

You already know that as you select words from the word list at the right of the Thesaurus dialog box, they appear in the Replace With Synonym field. If you then click on the [Look Up] button, Word for Windows will look up synonyms for that word. In fact, you could continue to step through synonyms, antonyms, or related words for as long as you like.

Notice that the Looked Up field at the upper left of the dialog box has an arrow to the right of it. If you decide to use the [Look Up] button to step through words, each word you step through is recorded by Word for Windows. You can go back to any of these words by clicking on the arrow to the right of the Looked Up field. When you do, you will see a list of the words you have looked up. Select one of the words, and Word for Windows immediately redisplays the synonyms for that word.

WHAT YOU NEED TO KNOW

Word for Windows includes a full-featured thesaurus, which you can use to improve your writing. In this lesson you should have learned the following:

☑ How to select and use a synonym

☑ How the thesaurus handles antonyms and related words

☑ How to change the declared language of selected text

☑ How you can step through words in the thesaurus

In the next lesson you will learn about another important Word for Windows tool—the spelling checker.

Lesson 25

Using the Spelling Checker

Let's face it—very few of us are perfect spellers. In fact, it is easy to misspell a word and not even realize it. If you aren't a perfect speller, you will be interested in using the spelling checker built into Word for Windows. In this lesson you will learn

- How to spell-check your entire document

- How to add a word to your dictionary

- How to spell-check a single word or a part of your document

- How to exclude parts of your document from being spell-checked

- How to change how the spelling checker works

CHECKING YOUR SPELLING

To check the spelling of your document, all you need to do is select the Spelling option from the Tools menu. Alternatively, you can select the ![ABC check] tool from the Standard toolbar or press **F7**. When you do, Word for Windows immediately starts checking the spelling within your document beginning at the cursor position. If a misspelled word is found, then you will see a dialog box similar to Figure 25.1:

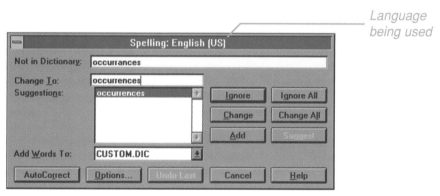

Figure 25.1 The Spelling dialog box.

Word for Windows is indicating the misspelled word and suggesting alternative spellings. The word which the program feels is the "best fit" is shown in the Change To field. Other possible replacements are shown in the word list under the Change To field. There are several options you can take at this point, all of which are selected by choosing one of the buttons in the dialog box, as detailed in Table 25.1:

Button	Function
Ignore	Ignores the word; no change is made.
Ignore All	Ignores this and all subsequent instances of the word.
Change	Changes the word to whatever is shown in the Change To field.
Change All	Changes this and all subsequent instances of the current word.
Add	Adds the word to the dictionary shown in the Add Words To list.
Suggest	If you type a word in the Change To field, and include either a question mark or an asterisk within the word (they function the same as DOS wildcard characters), clicking on this button provides suggested spellings.
Options...	Allows you to modify the parameters used by the spell checker. See later in this lesson for more information on this option.
Undo Last	Undoes the last correction you made. You can undo up to the last five corrections.
Cancel	Cancels the spell checking

Table 25.1 Spelling dialog box buttons.

You can also use the spelling checker to delete all occurrences of a misspelled word throughout a document. This is done by deleting the word in the Change To field. When you do this, the Change button is replaced with the Delete button, and Change All is replaced with Delete All Click on one of these buttons to carry out the corresponding action.

One of the other common errors which the spelling checker catches is duplicated words. For instance, let's suppose you entered **the the** within your document. In this instance, you would see the dialog box shown in Figure 25.2 when you ran the spell checker:

Figure 25.2 Spelling checker notes a repeated word.

Notice that only the Ignore , Delete , Suggest , Options... , and Cancel buttons are available, and there are no suggested spelling changes. Select the button that represents the action you want taken.

CHECKING SINGLE WORDS AND PARTS OF YOUR DOCUMENT

Word for Windows does not limit you to checking the spelling of your entire document. If you desire, you can check the spelling of a single word or of a text selection within your document.

To check the spelling of a single word, simply select the word. To check the spelling of a selection, make your selection. Then you can use any of the methods described earlier in this lesson to start the spelling checker. You can also press the **F7** key.

If Word for Windows did not discover any errors within the word or selected text, you will see the dialog box shown in Figure 25.3:

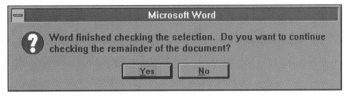

Figure 25.3 Select Yes to spell check the rest of the document.

LEAVING OUT PARTS OF YOUR DOCUMENT

In Section 4 of this book you learned how you can use templates and styles within your documents. One of the features of styles within Word for Windows is that you can specify how the spelling for specific paragraphs should be checked.

For instance, you can specify that a particular type of paragraph should be spell-checked using the Spanish dictionary or that it should never be spell-checked. To do this, review how you define and change styles. You first select Style from the Format menu, and then choose the style you want to modify. Click on the Modify... button, and you will see the dialog box shown in Figure 25.4:

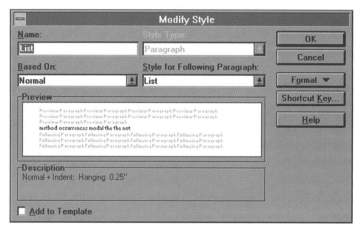

Figure 25.4 The Modify Style dialog box.

Select the style you want to change, and then click on the Format ▼ button. Select Language from the pull-down list, and you will see the dialog box shown in Figure 25.5:

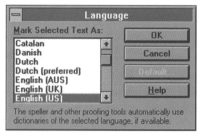

Figure 25.5 Language dialog box.

146

Here you can select the language that should be used when checking the spelling. At the top of the list is a *(no proofing)* choice. If you choose this, no spell-checking is done. This is a great option to use for paragraphs that may represent formats for catalog listings or program code lines.

If you desire, you can also change the language formatting of individual paragraphs by using the Language option from the Tools menu.

CHANGING OPTIONS

There are two ways you can change the options used by the spelling checker. The first is to click on the [Options...] button on the Spelling dialog box, described earlier in this lesson. This method is available only while you are actually checking spelling within a document, however. The other method is to choose Options from the Tools menu. Then, make sure the Spelling file card is selected. The Options dialog box then appears, as shown in Figure 25.6:

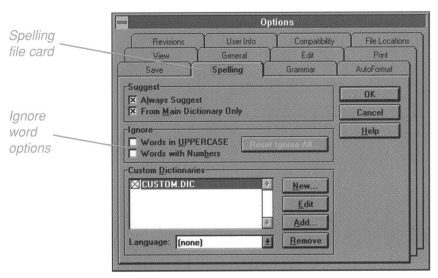

Spelling
file card

Ignore
word
options

Figure 25.6 Options dialog box showing Spelling file card.

Here, in the Ignore box, you can instruct Word for Windows to ignore words that are all capital letters and words that contain numbers. If you work with technical documents, you might find that these options come in handy. For instance, if you are working with a document that uses lots of acronyms (they are normally capitalized), then you might want to select the Words in UPPER-CASE check box. In this way, words such as IBM, ASPCA, NAACP, AFL-CIO, and ADA would all be ignored.

WHAT YOU NEED TO KNOW

In this lesson you have learned quite a bit about a powerful tool provided with Word for Windows. The spelling checker allows you to proof your spelling and even add your own dictionary entries. In particular, you have learned how to do the following:

- ☑ Spell-check your document
- ☑ Add words to a dictionary
- ☑ Use the spell checker to delete words in your document
- ☑ Check the spelling of a word or section of your document
- ☑ Omit parts of your document from being spell-checked
- ☑ Change spelling options

Lesson 26

Using the Grammar Checker

Perhaps the most powerful writing tool included with Word for Windows is the grammar checker. This powerful tool analyzes your document for common grammatical errors and makes suggestions on how you can improve your writing. In this lesson you will learn how you can use this tool. In particular, you will learn how to do the following:

- Check the grammar in your document
- Check the grammar in a part of your document
- Change the rules followed by the grammar checker

CHECKING YOUR DOCUMENT

To check how well your document stacks up against the grammar rules defined within Word for Windows, select the Grammar option from the Tools menu. When you do, Word for Windows immediately starts checking your document, beginning at the current cursor position. If a questionable phrase or word is found, you will see a dialog box similar to Figure 26.1:

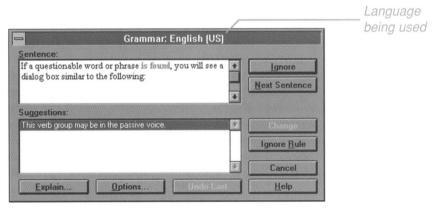

Figure 26.1 The Grammar dialog box.

Word for Windows is indicating what it sees as a possible problem. At the top of the dialog box is the sentence that Word for Windows is questioning, and at the bottom is the suggestion on how to make it better. The exact dialog box that is displayed depends on the type of error discovered. There are several options you can take at this point, all of which are selected by choosing one of the buttons in the dialog box:

Button	Function
Ignore	Ignores the problem; no change is made.
Next Sentence	Ignores the problem and any others that may exist within the sentence. Continues checking, beginning with the next sentence.
Change	Makes whatever change is being suggested. This option might not always be available, depending on the type of problem.
Ignore Rule	For the rest of the document, ignores the grammar rule that resulted in this problem being displayed.
Cancel	Cancels the grammar checking.
Explain...	Explains the grammar rule that Word for Windows thinks has been violated.
Options...	Allows you to modify the parameters and rules used by the grammar checker. See later in this lesson for more information on this option.
Undo Last	Undoes the last change made by the grammar checker.

Table 26.1 Grammar dialog box buttons.

Spell-checking is also included as part of the grammar checking. The same dialog boxes and guidelines discussed in Lesson 25 are used when a spelling error is discovered. Some people, however, may have already checked the spelling or they don't want to mix the grammar and spelling check. If you are one of these people, refer to the section later in this lesson, which deals with setting options for the grammar checker.

When the grammar check is complete, the program displays statistics about your document, similar to Figure 26.2:

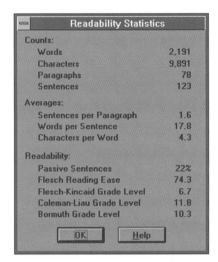

Figure 26.2 Grammar Checker Readability Statistics dialog box.

Obviously, these statistics will vary from document to document. The information here provides a readability analysis of your document according to several widely accepted sets of criteria. A complete explanation of these statistics is beyond the scope of this book, but you can get the general idea by examining the information in the dialog box. This information is provided by Word for Windows so you can determine, in general, if the readability of your document is appropriate for your target audience.

CHECKING PART OF YOUR DOCUMENT

If you want to check the grammar of only part of your document, highlight the part of the document you want to check and then start the grammar checker. The same checks and information are provided.

When Word for Windows has finished checking the text you have selected, you will see the dialog box shown in Figure 26.3:

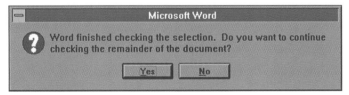

Figure 26.3 Select Yes to grammar check the rest of the document.

If you click on the [Yes] button, Word for Windows continues checking your document. If you click on [No], the readability statistics for the selection are displayed, and the grammar check is ended.

CHANGING GRAMMAR CHECKER RULES

The grammar checker operates by comparing each of the sentences in your document against a series of rules, which define how words generally appear for a given type of writing. Since the English language can be convoluted and archaic at times, the suggestions made by the program should not be considered infallible. In fact, Word for Windows provides a way you can modify the rules that are applied to your documents.

There are two ways you can change the options used by the grammar checker. The first is to click on the [Options...] button described earlier in this lesson. This method is available only while you are actually checking a document, however. The other method is to choose Options from the Tools menu. Then, make sure that Grammar file card is selected. The Options dialog box then appears, as shown in Figure 26.4:

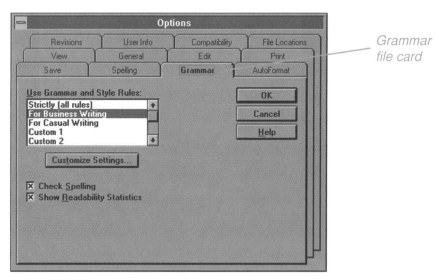

Figure 26.4 Options dialog box showing Grammar file card.

In general, this screen allows you to specify how stringent the grammar rules should be applied. Different levels of stringency are appropriate for different types of writing, and you can specify which type should be used in the Use Grammar and Style Rules box. One of the most commonly changed options is to instruct the grammar checker to not display any spelling errors it detects. This is done by selecting the Check Spelling check box. Another check box at the bottom of the dialog box allows you to turn the readability statistics on or off.

Finally, you can select the Customize Settings... button. When you do, Word for Windows displays the entire rule set used by the grammar checker, as shown in Figure 26.5:

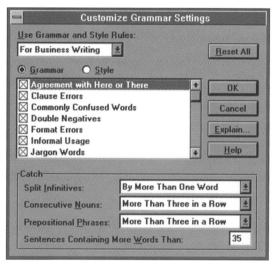

Figure 26.5 Customize Grammar Settings dialog box.

A complete explanation of these rules, their use, and the meaning of their settings is beyond the scope of this book. However, you can modify settings as you see fit, which will affect the type of problems which the grammar checker brings to your attention.

WHAT YOU NEED TO KNOW

Grammar checking is a tool you can use to improve your writing. While Word for Windows will not catch every grammatical error, it will present you with what it sees as problems and allow you to make changes. In this lesson you have learned how to

- ☑ Use the grammar checker
- ☑ Check only part of your document
- ☑ Display the readability statistics
- ☑ Change grammar rules

Lesson 27

Correcting What You Type

One of the newest tools in Word for Windows is called AutoCorrect. In some ways, this tool is closely akin to AutoText, which is discussed in Lesson 39. However, AutoCorrect has a different purpose—it helps you make corrections to your text as you type. In this lesson you will learn how to use this powerful tool. Specifically, you will learn the following:

- What AutoCorrect can do

- How to create an AutoCorrect entry

- How to use an AutoCorrect entry

- How to delete an AutoCorrect entry

Understanding AutoCorrect

To begin to understand what AutoCorrect can do, choose the AutoCorrect option from the Tools menu. When you do, you will see the AutoCorrect dialog box, shown in Figure 27.1.

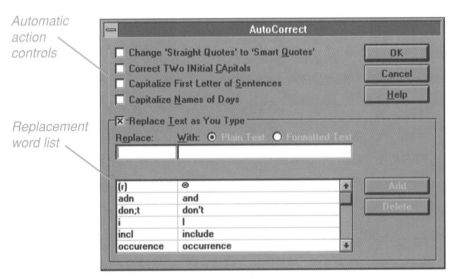

Figure 27.1 The AutoCorrect dialog box

154

There are two main parts to the AutoCorrect dialog box. The top part of the dialog box indicates items which AutoCorrect can change automatically. The bottom part of the dialog box is used for those items which you define for correction.

The items which AutoCorrect can change automatically include the following:

- *Change Straight Quotes to Smart Quotes* This option allows you to type as your normally would, but have Word for Windows automatically change your opening and closing quotes to smart quotes. *Smart quotes* are the name given to typographers quote marks which look different for opening and closing quotes. The quote marks used throughout this book are considered smart quotes. Here is an example of regular quotes, as opposed to smart quotes:

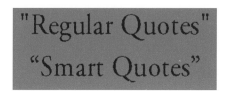

- *Correct TWo INitial CApitals* This is a great option if you are a fast typist, but you never quite get the SHIFT key released before typing the second letter of a word. If you select this item, Word for Windows will change the case of the second letter in the word automatically.

- *Capitalize First Letter of Sentences* If you hate to use the **SHIFT** key, this one is for you. When you turn on this option, Word for Windows will capitalize (as you type) the first letter of all sentences.

- *Capitalize Names of Days* The value of this option may be limited to some users, but others may benefit from it. As you type the name of a day of the week (such as Tuesday), Word for Windows will automatically capitalize the first letter of the word—even if you enter it in lowercase.

To select any of these options, simply click on the check box to the left of the option. An   in the check box indicates it is selected; an empty check box means that AutoCorrect will not perform the associated function.

The second major part of the AutoCorrect dialog box (the area titled Replace Text as You Type) is used to specify shorthand entries (similar to AutoText, discussed in Lesson 39) and identify common mistakes. For instance, during the writing of this book, I got tired of spelling out *Word for Windows* all the time. To do this quicker, I simply assigned an AutoCorrect entry that replaced the characters *ww* with the full text *Word for Windows*. As a result, I was able to type faster, and Word for Windows did a lot of the work.

While using AutoCorrect for shorthand notations is handy, you can also use it to correct common typing errors. For instance, suppose you commonly transpose characters—for instance, you type *teh* when you mean *the*. If you make an AutoCorrect entry for *teh,* replacing those characters with *the,* you will never have to worry about correcting those errors again.

CREATING AN AUTOCORRECT ENTRY

If you turn on the Replace Text as You Type option of AutoCorrect, you can add entries to the replacement list. These entries are stored within Word for Windows; they are available to all your documents. Adding an entry is very easy, but perhaps it is best to illustrate with a couple of examples. This first example shows how to use AutoCorrect as a type of shorthand.

Let's suppose you work for the Davis County Sheriff's Department, and you routinely generate memos and reports that require you to type this over and over again. Rather than do this, you can define an AutoCorrect entry to make your typing job much easier. To assign the name to an AutoCorrect entry, follow these steps:

1. Choose the AutoCorrect option from the Tools menu. You will see the AutoCorrect dialog box, shown earlier in Figure 27.1.

2. Decide on a shorthand version of your longer name. This short version cannot contain any spaces. For instance, you may decide to use *dc* to represent *Davis County Sheriff's Department.*

3. In the *Replace* field, type **dc** Press TAB to move to the next field.

4. In the *With* field, type **Davis County Sheriff's Department.** Note that if you had some text selected before you performed step 1, that text would already appear within the *With* field.

5. Select the [Add] button. If you choose an AutoCorrect entry that is already defined, you are asked to confirm that you want to overwrite the current definition. Click on the [Yes] button to do so.

6. Click on [OK] to close the AutoCorrect dialog box.

That's all there is to it. When you start typing, anytime you type **dc**, it is automatically replaced with *Davis County Sheriff's Department*. You save an incredible 31 keystrokes over typing out the longhand version of the name.

Another example of using AutoCorrect is in order. This one supposes that you want to use AutoCorrect to help you automatically correct your faulty typing. Suppose, for instance, that you can't ever seem to type *receive* properly. Instead, you always transpose the *e* and *i*, typing it as *recieve*. To have Word for Windows automatically correct your spelling for this common mistake, simply direct AutoCorrect to replace *recieve* with *receive*, using the same steps described above. Your typing will then be correct which ever way you spell it.

DELETING AN AUTOCORRECT ENTRY

There may come a time when you wish to delete an AutoCorrect entry. For instance, suppose you stopped working for the Davis County Sheriff's Department, and began working for the Davis County Search and Rescue Team. You can define a new AutoCorrect entry for your new department (as described earlier in this lesson), but you might also want to delete the old entry so it no longer consumes part of your system memory.

To review and delete AutoCorrect entries, you choose the AutoCorrect option from the Tools menu again. You will see the AutoCorrect dialog box (refer back to Figure 27.1), and you can select individual AutoCorrect entries from the list provided. If you decide that you no longer need the entry, simply click on the Delete button. The entry is immediately removed.

WHAT YOU NEED TO KNOW

AutoCorrect is one of the biggest time savers in Word for Windows. It allows you to correct automatically what you type as you type it. While this capability has been available with some add-on software in the past, it is now a part of Word 6.0 for Windows. You should now know how to do the following about AutoCorrect:

☑ Define an AutoCorrect entry

☑ Reuse an AutoCorrect entry by using the name again

☑ Expand an AutoCorrect entry in your document

☑ Delete an AutoCorrect entry

Lesson 28

Sorting Parts of Your Document

One of the frequently used tools included with Word for Windows is the sorting tool. Most often, this tool is used to place lists of information in a particular order. In this lesson you will learn how to use this tool, focusing on these areas:

- How to sort a group of paragraphs

- How to change sorting parameters

- The differences between alphanumeric and numeric sorting

SORTING PARAGRAPHS

When you are creating reports and manuals, you will often need to sort paragraphs of information. For instance, consider the following list of items:

> John's Bakery
> Carl's TV & Audio
> City Center Tours
> Quality Appliances
> Bay City Books
> Wilson's Aquatic Sports
> Hillside Drugs
> Sandra's Stationery

This is list of businesses is not in any particular order. Earlier in this book you learned how you can cut and paste text, and you could certainly arrange this list manually by using editing techniques. In this case, it would take you only a few moments. If the list of businesses grew longer, however, the manual arrangement method could take several hours. The sorting tool within Word for Windows allows you to sort any size list—large or small—within a matter of a few seconds. To do this, follow these steps:

1. Select the paragraphs you want sorted. (If you don't select the paragraphs you want sorted, Word for Windows assumes you want to sort all the paragraphs in your document.

2. Choose Sort Text from the Table menu; you will see the Sorting dialog box, shown in Figure 28.1.

3. Click on [OK], or press Enter.

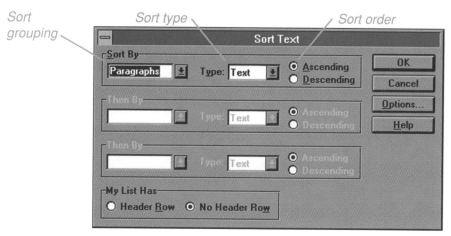

Figure 28.1 The Sort Text dialog box.

While this may seem really simplistic, no attempt has been made to make it that way—it really is easy. Most of the options within the Sorting dialog box can be safely ignored if you are only sorting paragraphs. If you are sorting tables, you can use sorting options that affect how your data is sorted within the tables, and the sorts can be much more complex. (Tables are covered in Section 7 of this book, although sorting tables is beyond the scope of this book.)

When the sorting is complete, your list of businesses will look like this:

> Bay City Books
> Carl's TV & Audio
> City Center Tours
> Hillside Drugs
> John's Bakery
> Quality Appliances
> Sandra's Stationery
> Wilson's Aquatic Sports

Even though most of the options within the Sorting dialog box can be safely ignored for performing simple sorts, there are two options that you might reasonably use on a regular basis. These are the options that control the sorting order and the type of sort you want Word for Windows to perform.

CONTROLLING THE SORTING ORDER

Take another look at the Sorting dialog box, shown in Figure 28.1. Notice that there are two options that allow you to specify if you will be sorting in ascending or descending order:

Select sort order

Ascending order simply means that the items a placed in order from lesser to greater, as in the following:

        123
        234
        345
        apple
        bingo
        Catskills

Notice that numbers are placed before letters, and everything is placed in the order 0–9 and A–Z.

Descending order is just the opposite; it means that items are placed in the reverse order:

        Catskills
        bingo
        apple
        345
        234
        123

In this instance, letters come before numbers, and items are placed in the order of Z–A and 9–0.

CONTROLLING THE TYPE OF SORT

If you look again at the Sorting dialog box (Figure 28.1), you will see that there is a field, near the middle of the dialog box, called Type:

Select type of sort

If you click on the arrow to the right of this field, you will discover that there are three types of sorts that Word for Windows can perform—Text, Number, and Date. You should take a moment to figure out what type of information you are asking Word for Windows to sort, and then make your choice accordingly. The following sections detail the effects of each choice you make in this part of the Sorting dialog box.

SORTING TEXT

Text is the default sorting type, since it applies to the broadest number of sorting cases. It simply means that information is sorted as already discussed earlier in the lesson. When you use this type of sort, every character in each paragraph is considered individually and compared to characters in the same position in other paragraphs.

When you choose Text sorting, there is a further option you can use to control how Word for Windows performs the sort. Once you have selected Text sorting, click on the Options... button. You will then see the dialog box shown in Figure 28.2.

Figure 28.2 *The Sort Options dialog box.*

The Case Sensitive option (in the middle of the dialog box) controls how upper- and lowercase characters are treated. If this option is selected, Word for Windows will treat upper- and lowercase characters differently. Thus, if you turned on case sensitivity, the following would be considered a sorted list:

    Air
    Angle
    Awesome
    aardvark
    absent
    arrange

Notice that all of the capital letters appeared before the lowercase letters. If you turn off case sensitivity, the list is sorted differently:

aardvark
absent
Air
Angle
arrange
Awesome

You should make your selection based on how you want the final list to appear.

SORTING NUMBERS

In some instances, an Alphanumeric sort might not acceptable for the type of information you want sorted. For instance, let's suppose you have the following short list you want sorted:

4385
324
90
234
123

If you sort it using the Alphanumeric sort type, it will end up like this:

123
234
324
4385
90

This is probably not the way you want the information sorted. The number 90 comes at the end of the list because 9 (the first character in the number) is greater than the first character in 4385. If you are sorting a list made up predominantly of numbers, you will want to specify Numbers as your type of sort. In this instance, Word for Windows treats individual paragraphs as numbers, meaning that your sort would turn out like this:

90
123
234
324
4385

This is the proper way for the information you want presented.

SORTING DATES

The final sorting type is a Date. This is a variation on the Numeric sort that results in dates being sorted properly. For instance, suppose you had the following dates in a list:

    1/1/56
    3/17/86
    6/11/56
    2/9/77
    8/19/79

If you used a numeric sort to sort them, your list would appear as follows:

    3/17/86
    2/9/77
    8/19/79
    6/11/56
    1/1/56

Notice that the sort was not done properly. In this case, Word for Windows took the first two sets of numbers in each date and performed a division (the slashes signify that the numbers should be divided) and then sorted the result. Thus, 3/17 results in .18, 2/9 results in .22, 8/19 results in .42, 6/11 results in .55, and 1/1 results in 1. In this order, the list is sorted numerically as far as Word for Windows is concerned.

However, if you used the Date sorting type, Word for Windows translates the slashes as date separator characters, and the list is sorted like this:

    1/1/56
    6/11/56
    2/9/77
    8/19/79
    3/17/86

Word for Windows will translate the information correctly whether you are using slashes, dashes, or a mix of the two. It will not sort them correctly if you have the dates spelled out, as in August 19, 1979.

WHAT YOU NEED TO KNOW

Sorting is a common operation that is made simple by the sorting tool included with Word for Windows. While many of your sorting operations can be completed within just a few seconds, Word for Windows provides options that allow you to perform more complex types of sorts. In this lesson you have learned about the key elements of sorting information. You have learned:

- ☑ How to sort paragraphs
- ☑ How to specify the sort order
- ☑ How to specify the type of sort to perform
- ☑ The differences between alphanumeric, numeric, and date sorting

In the next lesson you will learn about another handy tool within Word for Windows—hyphenation.

Lesson 29

Hyphenating Your Document

Hyphenation is a finishing touch that many people add to their documents. It is a process of breaking words between two lines so that each line can be more equal in length. When done manually, hyphenation can be an extremely time-consuming task. Word for Windows allows you to automate the task by providing a hyphenation tool. In this lesson you will learn how to use that tool. In particular, you will learn how:

- Hyphenation works in Word for Windows
- To hyphenate your entire document
- To hyphenate a part of your document
- To exclude parts of your document from being hyphenated
- To change how hyphenation works

UNDERSTANDING HYPHENATION

Basically, automatic hyphenation within Word for Windows is initiated by selecting Hyphenation from the Tools menu. Word for Windows then proceeds to analyze your document, making determinations as to where hyphens should be inserted. Actually, *optional hyphens* are inserted. This means you can later edit your document, and if a word no longer breaks across the end of a line, then the hyphen will not appear (even though it still exists in the document).

In general, you should only hyphenate your document as a final step before printing. This will save you both time and effort. If you find you need to make extensive changes to your document later, you might want to remove all the optional hyphens previously placed in your document by Word for Windows. This is done by searching and replacing them, using the techniques learned in Lesson 13, "Finding and Replacing Text." You simply use the special code to search for optional hyphens, and then leave the replacement text field blank. This way they are removed from your document.

HYPHENATING YOUR DOCUMENT

To begin the hyphenation process, select the Hyphenation option from the Tools menu. When you do, Word for Windows displays the Hyphenation dialog box, which is shown in Figure 29.1.

Hyphenation
options

Hyphenation

☐ <u>A</u>utomatically Hyphenate Document   OK
☐ Hyphenate Words in <u>C</u>APS   Cancel

Hyphenation <u>Z</u>one: ⎸0.25"⎹ ▲▼   <u>M</u>anual...
<u>L</u>imit Consecutive Hyphens To: ⎸No Limit⎹ ▲▼   <u>H</u>elp

Figure 29.1 The Hyphenation dialog box.

There are two types of hyphenation you can perform in Word for Windows. The first, automatic hyphenation, results in Word for Windows making all the hyphenation decisions for you. This is accomplished by clicking on the Automatically Hyphenate Document check box and then clicking on ⎸ OK ⎹

While automatic hyphenation may be acceptable for short documents, you will probably want to use manual hyphenation (the other type of hyphenation) for longer documents where you may feel that Word for Windows might make some wrong choices. To hyphenate a document manually, click on the ⎸ Manual... ⎹ button.

Word for Windows then switches to Page Layout viewing mode (if you are not already using it) and immediately starts checking your document to determine where hyphenation is appropriate. Before making a change, however, you are asked to confirm it. When a word that can potentially be hyphenated is located, you will see a dialog box similar to that shown in Figure 29.2.

Syllable separators

Suggested hyphen

Figure 29.2 The Manual Hyphenation dialog box.

Word for Windows is indicating the word that can be hyphenated and suggesting places where it can be hyphenated. Within the Hyphenated At field, the cursor is located where Word for Windows thinks the word would best be hyphenated. If you want to move the hyphenation point, use the **LEFT ARROW** and **RIGHT ARROW** keys or click on the location within the word. You then have three choices, which are selected by using the buttons at the bottom of the dialog box. as shown in Table 29.1.

Button	Operation
Yes	Perform the hyphenation at the indicated position
No	Don't hyphenate this word
Cancel	Cancel the hyphenation process

Table 29.1 Buttons available for manual hyphenation.

When you click on the Yes or No buttons, Word for Windows proceeds to the next word that can be hyphenated, where you again have the opportunity to review the decision. When the hyphenation is complete, Word for Windows will inform you with the dialog box shown in Figure 29.3:

Figure 29.3 Notice that hyphenation is complete.

HYPHENATING SINGLE WORDS AND PARTS OF YOUR DOCUMENT

Word for Windows does not limit you to hyphenating your entire document. If you desire, you can hyphenate a single word or a selection of text in your document. In either case, all you need to do before selecting Hyphenation from the Tools menu is to select the word or text selection you want to hyphenate. You can then automatically or manually hyphenate the selection, as previously described.

If you decide to hyphenate a text selection larger than a single word, and you complete the hyphenation process, Word for Windows will display the dialog box shown in Figure 29.4:

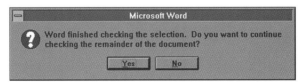

Figure 29.4 Select Yes to hyphenate the rest of the document.

LEAVING OUT PARTS OF YOUR DOCUMENT

There are two ways that Word for Windows allows you to control which parts of your documents are processed by the hyphenation tool. One way involves use of the Hyphenation dialog box, and the other involves the use of styles and languages.

One of the most obvious types of words you would not want to hyphenate is capitalized words—those in which every letter is uppercase. Typically, these are acronyms or initials, which are best kept on one line. For instance, you wouldn't want to hyphenate words such as NORAD or ASCII. To control hyphenation of these words, you use the Hyphenate CAPS option from the Hyphenation dialog box:

☐ **Hyphenate Words in CAPS**

If this check box is selected, uppercase words are checked and possibly hyphenated by Word for Windows. If the check box is not selected, they are ignored. For the most part, you will probably want to make sure this option is off.

In Section 4 of this book you learned how you can use templates and styles within your documents. One of the features of styles within Word for Windows is that you can specify how the writing tools (including hyphenation) affect specific paragraphs within your document.

For instance, you can specify that a particular type of paragraph should be hyphenated using a Spanish dictionary, or that it should never be hyphenated. To do this, review how you define and change styles. You first select Style from the Format menu and then choose the style you want to modify. Click on the Modify... button, and you will see the Modify Style dialog box, shown in Figure 29.5.

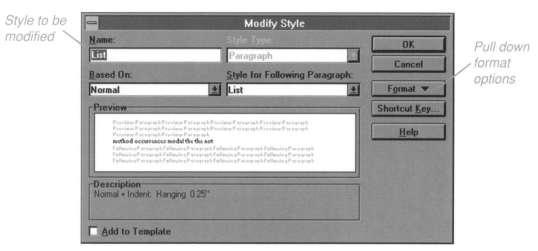

Style to be modified

Pull down format options

Figure 29.5 The Modify Style dialog box.

Click on the [Format ▼] button, select Language from the pull-down list, and you will see the dialog box shown in Figure 29.6:

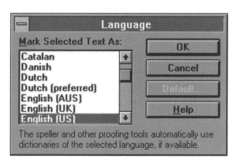

Figure 29.6 The Language dialog box.

Here you can select the language that should be used when hyphenating your document. At the top of the list is a (**no proofing**) choice. If you choose this, no hyphenation is done on any paragraph formatted with that particular style.

If you desire, you can also change the language formatting of individual paragraphs by using the Language option from the Tools menu.

UNDERSTANDING THE HYPHENATION ZONE

Word for Windows uses what is called a *hyphenation zone* when it hyphenates your documents. You probably noticed in the Hyphenation dialog box (Figure 29.1) that there is a field that indicates the current hyphenation zone:

The hyphenation zone can be changed to affect how Word for Windows implements this tool. The default hyphenation zone is 0.25 inches, meaning that if there is over 0.25 inches of white space (empty space) left at the end of a line, Word for Windows will attempt to hyphenate the first word on the following line. You can set the hyphenation zone to any value between 0.1 inch and 22 inches.

You might need to experiment with the hyphenation zone to determine the value that is best for your writing and page layout. In general, the lower the value used for the hyphenation zone, the more Word for Windows will attempt to hyphenate words. If you don't want a lot of hyphens, then you should set a higher hyphenation zone value.

LIMITING HYPHENATION OVERKILL

Traditionally, when you manually hyphenate your document (by hand, without the aid of Word for Windows), you must make sure that too many lines in your document don't end with a hyphen. If they do, then readers will find the text choppy and will be easily distracted by all the hyphens. To guard against this, Word for Windows allows you to specify how many lines in a row can end with a hyphen. This is done from the following portion of the Hyphenation dialog box:

By default, Word for Windows has no limit. This means that there is no checking done, and it is theoretically possible for every line in your document to be hyphenated. You can change this value to anything between 1 and 32,767. For instance, if you don't want over four consecutive lines to end in hyphens, you would set this value to 4.

In reality, it is very unlikely that you will need to set this option. It is a rare circumstance when a distractingly large number of lines end in hyphens. You might want to hyphenate with no limit set, and if you discover a problem that manifests itself with a given document, hyphenate again with a lower setting.

WHAT YOU NEED TO KNOW

In this lesson you have learned how you can use the Word for Windows hyphenation tool. This tool, when used effectively, can add to the professional appearance of your documents. In particular, you have learned how to

- ☑ Hyphenate your document
- ☑ Hyphenate only a portion of your document
- ☑ Omit parts of your document from being hyphenated
- ☑ Use the hyphenation zone

Lesson 30

Printing Envelopes

Word for Windows is often used for business communications. Letters, memos, reports, fliers, and all sorts of documents need to be created and distributed. Word for Windows provides a special tool that allows you to create and print envelopes easily. This lesson covers the use of this tool. You will learn how to

- Create an envelope
- Modify the return address
- Change the envelope options
- Change the printing options
- Print the envelope

CREATING AN ENVELOPE

In Word for Windows, an envelope consists of two distinct parts. The first is the return address, which appears in the upper-left corner of the envelope. The other is the delivery address, which appears in the center of the envelope. The arrangement of these elements on the envelope is shown in Figure 30.1.

Figure 30.1 An example envelope.

Word for Windows allows you to specify easily what belongs in each of these two parts of the envelope. To do so, simply select Envelopes and Labels from the Tools menu. You will then see the Envelopes and Labels dialog box, shown in Figure 30.2.

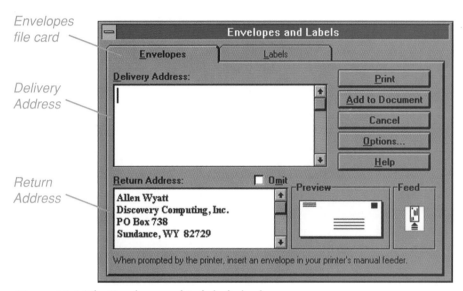

Figure 30.2 *The Envelopes and Labels dialog box.*

Notice that there are two parts to this dialog box, each depicted by a file card. Make sure you are looking at the Envelopes file card; your screen should appear very similar to the dialog box shown in Figure 30.2. (The Labels file card will be covered in detail in Lesson 31, "Printing Labels." How the dialog box actually appears on your screen might differ a bit, since Word for Windows always attempts to detect and provide as much information as possible. For instance, if you are writing a letter, Word for Windows will examine your document, beginning at the top of the file, and try to determine the delivery address. If it feels it can do so, it will show the delivery address in the Envelopes and Labels dialog box.

You can modify the delivery address and the return address as you desire, and even leave off the return address by selecting the Omit check box in the middle of the dialog box. When you are satisfied with your envelope, you can print it, as described later in this lesson.

How to Change Your Return Address

A default return address is maintained for you by Word for Windows. You can change it (outside of the envelope tool) by selecting Options from the Tools menu. When you do, make sure you have selected the User Info file card, and you will see the Options dialog box appear, similar to the one shown in Figure 30.3.

User Info
file card

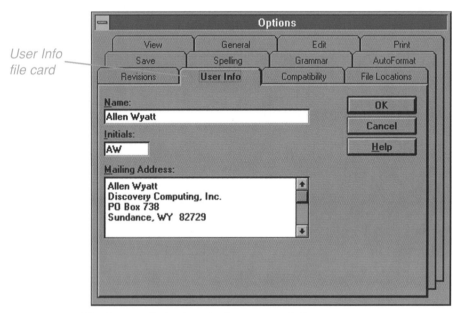

Figure 30.3 *The Options dialog box displaying User Info.*

In the Mailing Address portion of the dialog box, you can specify what you want used as a return address. Make any changes you desire and click on ⬛ OK

Changing the Envelope Options

At the beginning of this lesson you learned that there were two main parts to an envelope. Word for Windows allows you a great deal of freedom in placing these items on the physical envelope. In addition, you can specify the type of envelope you want to print. All of these aspects of your envelope are controlled through the Envelope Options dialog box. To access this dialog box, first go to the Envelope and Labels dialog box, as shown in Figure 30.2. Then either click on the ⬛ Options... button or in the preview area of the dialog box. You will then see the Envelope Options dialog box, shown in Figure 30.4.

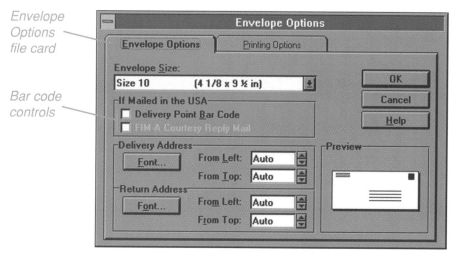

Envelope
Options
file card

Bar code
controls

Figure 30.4 *The Envelope Options dialog box*

SELECTING AN ENVELOPE

The first part of the Envelope Options dialog box allows you to specify what type of envelope you are using. Word for Windows supports the most common US and international envelope sizes, and gives you the option of specifying a custom size. The choices you can make here include the envelope sizes listed in Table 30.1.

US Sizes	International Sizes
Monarch (3 1/8 x 7 1/2")	C4 (229 x 324mm)
Size 6 (3 5/8 x 6 1/2")	C5 (162 x 229mm)
Size 9 (3 7/8 x 8 7/8")	C6 (114 x 162mm)
Size 10 (4 1/8 x 9 1/2")	C65 (114 x 229mm)
Size 11 (4 1/2 x 10 3/8")	DL (110 x 220mm)
Size 12 (4 3/4 x 11")	

Table 30.1 *Envelope sizes supported by Word for Windows.*

After you have specified an envelope size, notice that the sample envelope shown in the preview area (lower-right corner of the dialog box) changes to reflect your selection. This area is updated every time you make a choice that changes how the envelope looks.

UNDERSTANDING POSTAL BAR CODES

Word for Windows allows you to include either of two bar codes on your envelope. The two check boxes in the middle of the Envelope Options dialog box allow you to do this:

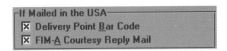

Both bar codes are only applicable if the letter is intended for use within the United States. The Delivery Point Bar Code option results in the addition of a bar code strip right above the delivery address. This bar code is read by US Postal Service automation equipment and helps the letter reach its destination quicker. In addition, some classes of mail are eligible for postage discounts if the bar code is included.

If you choose to include the Delivery Point Bar Code, you can then choose to include the FIM-A Courtesy Reply Mail bar code. This appears just to the left of the stamp area on the envelope, and informs the postal equipment that the envelope is return mail—the type where the recipient is paying the postage. Figure 30.5 shows an example of an envelope layout with both the Delivery Point Bar Code and FIM-A Courtesy Reply Mail options selected.

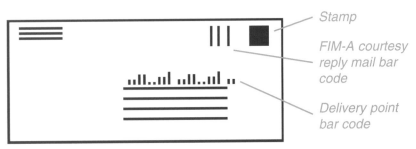

Figure 30.5 A sample envelope.

POSITIONING THE ELEMENTS OF THE ENVELOPE

Besides the envelope type and the inclusion of postal bar codes, in the lower-left portion of the Envelope Options dialog box, you can specify the font and location for both the Delivery Address and Return Address. While Word for Windows normally does a very good job of positioning these envelope elements, you might have a need to move them manually. For instance, you might have a specially printed envelope that has something already printed on it—something you don't want Word for Windows to print over.

When you have finished making your adjustments to the envelope, you can click on the [OK] button to return to the Envelopes and Labels dialog box.

CHANGING THE PRINTING OPTIONS

Word for Windows allows you to control how the envelope is printed on your particular printer. This is done by accessing the Printing Options dialog box. To access this dialog box, first go to the Envelopes and Labels dialog box (see Figure 30.2) and then either click on the Feed area (lower-right corner of the dialog box) or click on the [Options...] button and select the Printing Options file card. Regardless of which way you do it, you should see the Envelope Options dialog box, shown in Figure 30.6.

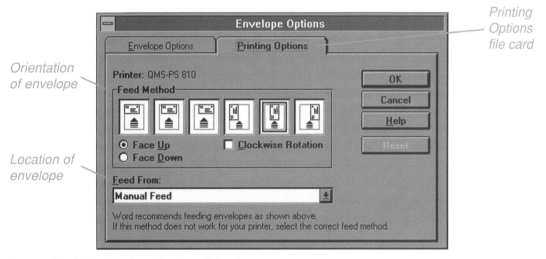

Figure 30.6 *The Envelope Options dialog box*

This example of the Printing Options dialog box is what is displayed if you are using a PostScript printer. If you are using a different type of printer, your dialog box will differ, to reflect the possible options for your particular type of printer.

In the choices at the top of the dialog box, choose how you want to orient the envelope when you feed it into the printer. At the bottom of the dialog box, choose how the printer will receive the envelope. For instance, you might want to indicate that you will feed the envelope manually (this is the default setting), or that you have a supply of envelopes being fed to the printer automatically.

When you have finished making your adjustments to the envelope, you can click on the [OK] button to return to the Envelopes and Labels dialog box.

PRINTING THE ENVELOPE

The final step is to print your envelope. This is done from the Envelopes and Labels dialog box, as previously shown in Figure 30.2. Word for Windows provides two ways to print your envelope. The first is actually to print the envelope to your printer. This is good if you are only printing a single copy of the envelope. To do this, choose the [Print] button.

The other method of printing your envelope involves inserting it into your document, and then printing it as you would any other document. This is done by choosing the [Add to Document] button. This option is best if you are going to print multiple copies of the same envelope, or if you will be using the mail merge portion of Word for Windows to print the envelopes. (Mail merge is one of the advanced topics that are beyond the scope of this book.)

No matter which printing method you choose, when you click on either the [Print] or [Add to Document] dialog box, you might see the dialog box shown in Figure 30.7:

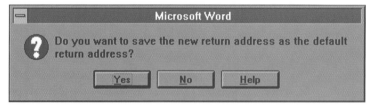

Figure 30.7 Select Yes to change saved return address.

This dialog box appears only if you have made changes to your return address. If you click on [Yes], your mailing address information is updated, as described earlier in this lesson. If you click on [No], Word for Windows assumes that the return address change is applicable to this envelope only.

WHAT YOU NEED TO KNOW

In this lesson you have learned how you can create and print envelopes using the envelope tool in Word for Windows. This tool allows you very nearly to automate the creation of your envelopes. After completing this lesson, you should know how to do the following:

- ☑ Create an envelope
- ☑ Change your return address
- ☑ Change options that affect the layout of the envelope
- ☑ Change options that affect how the envelope prints
- ☑ Print the envelope

In the next lesson you will learn about printing labels—a capability that is close in concept to envelope printing.

Lesson 31

Printing Labels

In Lesson 30 you learned how you can use Word for Windows to print envelopes. This lesson discusses a closely related tool that allows you to print labels. These labels can be used for mailing labels or virtually any other purpose you desire. This lesson will teach you how to

- Create a label
- Choose a label type
- Define a custom label
- Print your labels

CREATING A LABEL

In Word for Windows, labels are an extension of the table capabilities discussed in Section 7. While it is a bit premature to discuss tables in detail, you should understand that when you create a sheet of labels in Word for Windows, you are creating a table, in which each cell represents an individual label.

To begin working with labels, select Envelopes and Labels from the Tools menu. You will then see the Envelopes and Labels dialog box. Make sure that the Labels file card is selected, and the dialog box will appear, as shown in Figure 31.1.

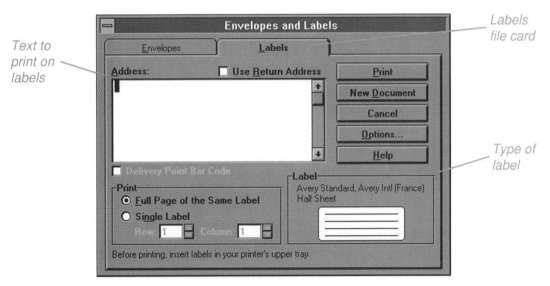

Figure 31.1 *The Envelopes and Labels dialog box.*

Basically, the steps in designing a label are simple:

1. Select a label

2. Indicate what should be printed on the labels

3. Print the labels

Selecting a label type will be covered in the next section, and printing the labels is covered near the end of this lesson. Step 2, choosing something to print on the labels, is easy. All you need to do is type the information in the Address area of the Envelopes and Labels dialog box.

Don't be fooled by the area name (Address) into thinking that Word for Windows will only handle address labels. Actually, you can print anything you want on the labels. Simply type the information it in, and it will appear on each label.

Recognizing that you might want to create a group of return address labels, Word for Windows allows you to include your return address on the label quickly. Select the Use Return Address option at the top of the dialog box. When you do, your address is included in the Address area of the dialog box. If you want to change your default return address, refer to Lesson 30, "Printing Envelopes."

HOW TO PICK A LABEL TYPE

Word for Windows supports many different types of labels. All of these aspects of your envelope are controlled through the Label Options dialog box. To access this dialog box, first go to the Envelope and Labels dialog box, as shown in Figure 31.1. Then either click on the [Options...] button or in the preview area (lower-right corner) of the dialog box. You will see the Label Options dialog box, shown in Figure 31.2.

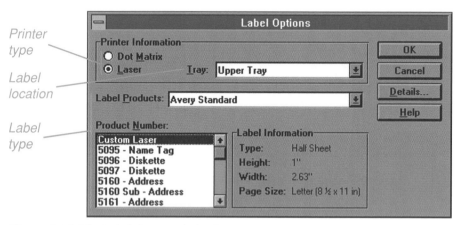

Figure 31.2 The Label Options dialog box.

The printer information, at the top of the dialog box, should already be set to what you will be using for your printer. If not, make a change so that it reflects the type of printer you will be using. This is important, since it affects the other choices available on the dialog box.

Next, indicate who makes your labels. Word for Windows includes labels created by the leading label manufacturers. The example in Figure 31.2 shows that Avery Standard labels are selected. You can select other label manufacturers by using the pull-down list for this field.

The printer information and the label manufacturer will determine which types of labels you can select. Labels are listed by their product ID, which is assigned by the manufacturer. For instance, if you are using Avery labels, the product ID is prominently displayed on the label package, typically in the front upper right corner. Match this ID with the list of available labels, and Word for Windows will take care of all the label formatting.

When you are through selecting your label type, you can click on the [OK] button to return to the Envelopes and Labels dialog box.

DESIGNING A CUSTOM LABEL

Even though Word for Windows includes quite a few different predefined label types, you can still create your own custom labels. This is done by first displaying the Label Options dialog box (as shown in Figure 31.2), and then making sure that the Custom label (Custom Laser or Custom Dot Matrix) is chosen in the Product Number list. This is the label chosen in Figure 31.2.

Next, click on the [Details...] button. Word for Windows then displays a dialog box similar to the one shown in Figure 31.3. The name of this dialog box, as shown in the title bar, will depend on the label chosen in the Product Number list of the Label Options dialog box.

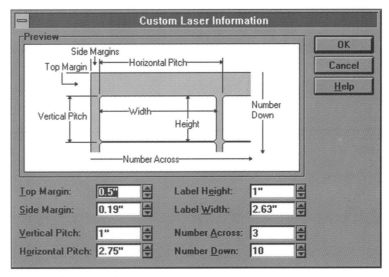

Figure 31.3 The label definition dialog box.

You can adjust the label positioning and spacing information as you desire. The preview area, at the top of the dialog box, indicates what your adjusted labels look like. When you have finished making changes, click on the [OK] button to return to the Label Options dialog box.

PRINTING THE LABELS

The final step is to print your labels. This is done from the Envelopes and Labels dialog box, as previously shown in Figure 31.1. Before you chose your printing method (there are two of them, covered shortly), you should specify what you want to print. This is done in the lower-left corner of the dialog box:

The default is to print a full page of labels. You can also, however, choose to print only a specific label on the sheet. If you choose this latter option, you must indicate the row and column of the label you want to print.

Word for Windows provides two ways to print your labels. The first is to print them to your printer. This is good if you are only printing a single pass of the labels, or if you are printing a single label out of an entire sheet. To print directly to the printer, choose the Print button.

The other method of printing your labels involves creating a new document that contains a table defining the labels. This is done by choosing the New Document button. The New Document button is available only if you are printing complete sheets of labels.

Once the new document is created, you can print it as you would any other Word for Windows document. This option is best if you are going to print multiple copies of the labels, or if you will be using the mail merge portion of Word for Windows to print the labels. (Mail merge is one of the advanced topics beyond the scope of this book.)

Another handy use for choosing the New Document button is to create a sheet of blank labels that you can fill in later. When you do this, Word for Windows creates a single-page document that contains nothing but an empty table. Each cell in the table defines an individual label on the sheet. You can place information in each cell, and then print the document at a later time.

WHAT YOU NEED TO KNOW

In this lesson you have learned how to create and print labels using the label tool in Word for Windows. This tool allows you to create one or 100 labels quickly and easily. After completing this lesson, you should know how to

☑ Create a label

☑ Choose a label type

☑ Design a custom label

☑ Print your labels

ADDING PIZZAZZ

In Section 3, "Basic Formatting Skills," you learned how you can use Word for Windows to control the appearance of your text. In addition to changing how characters, paragraphs, and margins appear, however, Word for Windows allows you to add borders, graphics, drawings, and charts. Each of these allows you to add character and style, which sets your documents apart from those that are created with run-of-the-mill word processors.

Lesson 32 *Bordering Your Text*

Lesson 33 *Adding Graphics*

Lesson 34 *Adding Drawings*

Lesson 35 *Using Microsoft Graph*

Lesson 32

Bordering Your Text

By this point you should be fairly comfortable with using Word for Windows. You know how to enter, edit, and save text. You also know how to print your documents and use some of the writing tools provided with Word for Windows. In this lesson you will learn how you can add some character to your text. This lesson teaches you:

- How to add borders around your text
- How to change the border type
- How to add drop shadows

ADDING A BORDER

Word for Windows allows you to add borders around one or a group of paragraphs in your text. This is done by first selecting the paragraphs, or by positioning the cursor in the single paragraph you want to border, and then selecting the Borders and Shading option from the Format menu. You will see the Paragraph Borders and Shading dialog box; make sure that the Borders file card is selected, as shown in Figure 32.1:

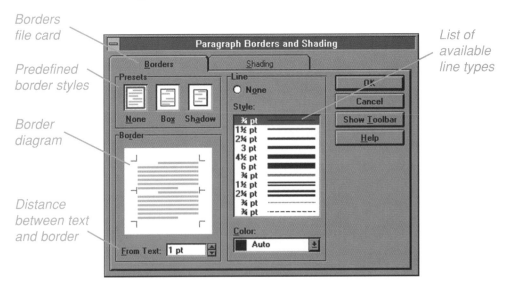

Figure 32.1 Adding paragraph borders.

Adding the border is as simple as selecting a line type from those in the center of the dialog box, and then clicking on the depiction of the box in the preset area in the bottom left corner of the dialog box. When you then click on [OK], the border is added.

Take a look at the Paragraph Borders and Shading dialog box again. Notice that you can use any of up to 11 line types (12, if you count None as a line type). Each of these types provides a different effect for the box. Notice, also, that you can add a *drop shadow* to your paragraphs. This is done by selecting the rightmost preset (Shadow) in the Presets area.

Finally, you can adjust how close the lines used in the border are to the text in the paragraph. This is done by adjusting the value in the From Text field.

BORDERING ONLY PART OF A PARAGRAPH

Notice that in the lower-left corner of the Border dialog box is an area labeled Border. Using this box, you can control where Word for Windows places borders around your paragraph. If you choose the presets at the top of the dialog box, these borders are set automatically. However, you can control individual borders by selecting the border you desire and then specifying a line type.

To select a border, click on the part of the diagram that contains the border you want to set. For instance, if you want to set a border above your paragraph, click on the line just above the example text. Two little arrows appear at both sides, indicating which line is selected.

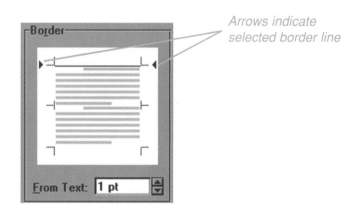

Arrows indicate selected border line

You can then click on a line type, and the border is changed. Choose another border and line type and that change is reflected. When you are satisfied with how your borders appear, click on the [OK] button.

ADJUSTING APPEARANCES

When you add a box or a border to your paragraphs, Word for Windows tries to keep the text margins of the paragraph stable. In other words, the border is drawn around the outside of the paragraph, leaving the text margins where they were. This can, unfortunately, cause your boxed text to look a bit odd in comparison to other elements on your page.

In order to overcome this, you might need to adjust your text margins so they allow for the size of the box. For instance, if you are using a thin line (about one point wide) and you have placed the border four points from the text, then you might need to increase the left and right text margins by five points. This positions the border so it lines up with the other margins on the page.

As you are working with borders and how they relate to margins, you will probably want to change to Page Layout viewing mode. You can even magnify the text so it is as large as possible. This allows you to view precisely where both the margins and the border are placed.

SHADING A PARAGRAPH

Another attribute that Word for Windows allows you to add to paragraphs is shading. This is done by choosing the Borders and Shading option from the Format menu, after which you will see the Paragraph Borders and Shading dialog box. Select the Shading file card, and the dialog box will appear as shown in Figure 32.2:

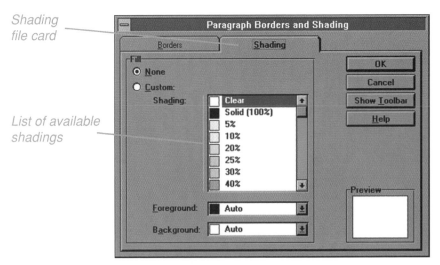

Figure 32.2 Shading a paragraph.

Here you can choose how you want the area within your borders filled. (You don't, actually need any borders to add shading. Just choose the shading option, and Word for Windows adds the shading as if you had borders on the paragraph.)

In the Shading box, you can choose one of 26 different patterns to use. The Foreground and Background boxes allow you to specify which colors are used for the dots or lines in the pattern (foreground) and the space not used by the dots or lines (background). By experimenting with these settings, you can achieve some interesting shading effects.

WHAT YOU NEED TO KNOW

Word for Windows allows you to spice up your text by adding borders and shading to individual paragraphs. In this lesson you have learned how to

- ☑ Add borders to one or more paragraphs
- ☑ Use the border presets to create boxes or drop-shadow boxes
- ☑ Adjust the distance between the border and the text within the border
- ☑ Add shading to your text

Lesson 33

Adding Graphics

While many types of documents might use just text, other documents require the addition of graphics, charts, and drawings to convey the information intended. This lesson is the first of three that address how to add these extra touches to your documents. In this lesson you will learn:

- What graphics files are

- How to add them to your document

- How to adjust how text behaves in relation to the graphic

WHAT ARE GRAPHICS FILES?

Simply stated, a *graphics file* is nothing more than a disk file containing a picture. That is where the simplicity ends, however. That is because there are literally dozens (if not hundreds) of ways that the picture can be stored in the file. While this book is not designed to address different graphic file formats, you should know that Word for Windows will read and allows you to use pictures stored in several different formats:

File Extension	Format
AI	PostScript AI
ATT	AT&T Group 4
BMP	Windows Bitmap
CAL	CALS Raster
CGM	Computer Graphics Metafile
CLP	Windows CLP
CMP, JPC	JPEG Compressed
CPR	Knowledge CPR
CUT	Dr. Halo
DBX	DataBeam
DIB	Windows or OS/2 DIB
DRW	Micrografx Designer/Draw

Table 33.1 Graphics file types. (continued on next page)

File Extension	Format
DXF	AutoCAD DXF File
ED5	EDMICS
EPS	Encapsulated PostScript
FAX	Fax Type
GCA	IBM GOCA
GED	Wicat
GEM	GEM Metafile
GIF	CompuServe Graphic
HGL	HP Graphics Language
ICA	IBM IOCA
ICO	Windows Icon
IFF	Amiga
IGF	Inset Graphics Format
IMG	GEM Paint
KFX	Kofax Group 4
MAC	MacPaint
MSP	Microsoft Paint
P10	Tektronix P10
PCD	PhotoCD
PCL	HP LaserJet
PCT	Macintosh or Windows PICT
PCX	PC Paintbrush
PGL	HP Plotter
PIC	Lotus 1-2-3 Graphics
PIX	Inset PIX Format
PLT	AutoCAD Plot File
RAS, SUN	Sun Raster
RLE	Windows or OS/2 RLE
SBP	StoryBoard PIC
TGA	Targa
TIF	Tagged Image File Format
TXT	ASCII Text
WMF	Windows or OS/2 Metafile
WPG	DrawPerfect

Table 33.1 *Graphics file types. (continued from previous page)*

These formats represent the majority of the graphics file formats available. These files can either be generated by you or you can get them from any of a number of other sources. For instance, you may use PC Paintbrush, and save your drawing in PCX file format. Word for Windows will read it directly into your document, placing it wherever you desire.

ADDING A GRAPHIC TO YOUR DOCUMENT

There are two methods you can use to add a graphic to your file. The first method is to place it directly into the text. The other is to use a *frame,* which provides you with additional control over how the graphic is treated in your document.

To add a graphic directly into text, simply position the cursor where you want the graphic placed. Then choose the Picture option from the Insert menu. You will see the Insert Picture dialog box, as shown in Figure 33.1:

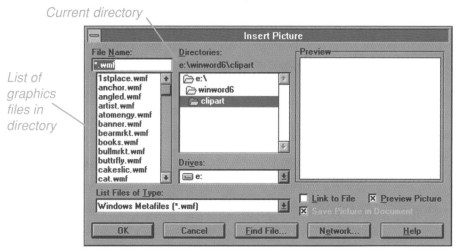

Figure 33.1 The Insert Picture dialog box.

(You may or may not see all the buttons at the bottom of the dialog box, depending on your Windows configuration.) Use the Insert Picture dialog box to select the graphics file you want inserted. When you click on the ⬛ OK ⬛ button, the picture is placed in the text.

The other method is to create a *frame,* into which the graphic file is placed. A frame, while not limited to just graphics (it can contain text, as well), is ideally suited to displaying images. This is because you can move the frame—and the graphic it contains—independently of the text that surrounds it. Thus, you can size the frame and allow text to flow freely around it.

To place a frame in your document, choose the Frame option from the Insert menu. Word for Windows will switch to Page Layout viewing mode so you can insert the frame. The mouse cursor then changes to a small plus sign (some people call them crosshairs). Position the cursor at one corner of where you want the frame, and then click and hold the left mouse button. As you move the mouse, the size of the frame grows. When you are satisfied with the frame size, release the mouse button. The frame is now positioned within your document. You can move the frame by selecting an edge with the mouse cursor and dragging it to any location desired.

To place the graphic within the frame, place the cursor within the frame and then insert a picture, as was discussed earlier in this section.

CHANGING THE SIZE OF A GRAPHIC OR FRAME

If you click on either a graphic or a frame, you will see that small squares appear at the corners and around the edge of the graphic or frame. These are called *handles*. These handles are used to change the size of the graphic or frame. To do this, you simply point to one of the handles, click and hold the left mouse button, and drag the mouse until the frame or graphic is the desired size. When you release the mouse button, the frame or graphic remains at the new size.

Another way to size a picture is to use the Picture option from the Format menu. When you choose this, you will see the Picture dialog box as shown in Figure 33.2:

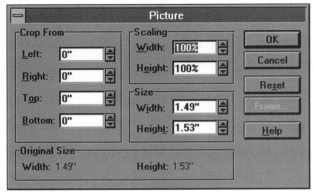

Figure 33.2 The Picture Dialog box.

This dialog box allows you to specify the cropping (how much of the image is cut off), as well as the scaling and size of the image. By using these controls, you can set the image size so it appears exactly as you want it to.

Note: A quick way to scale a graphic or frame is to drag it by one of its handles with your mouse. A quick way to crop (or add white space around) a graphic or frame is to press SHIFT *while dragging.*

WRAPPING TEXT AROUND A FRAME

If you have placed your graphic within a frame, you can control how text flows in relation to the frame. For instance, you can instruct Word for Windows to allow the text to flow around the frame or to not flow around it. If you choose to have it flow around it, then how you position and size the frame determines where the graphic appears.

To choose how the frame is formatted, select the frame and then choose the Frame option from the Format menu. If you don't select the frame first, then the menu option will not be available. When you choose the Frame option, you will see the Frame dialog box, shown in Figure 33.3:

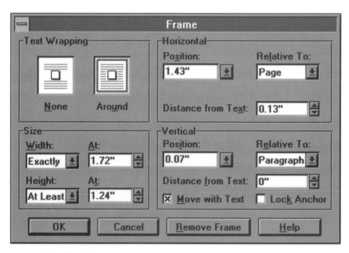

Figure 33.3 The Frame Dialog box.

This dialog box allows you to specify the size and positioning (horizontal and vertical) of the frame. You can also indicate, in the upper-left corner, how you want text to flow in relation to the frame. You will want to experiment with the settings in this dialog box so that you are pleased with how the frame appears in your document.

Note: You can also open the Frame dialog box by double-clicking on the edge of a frame.

DELETING A GRAPHIC OR FRAME

As you learned in Lesson 8, pressing DEL results in text being cleared, while pressing CTRL-X cuts it from your document but places it in the Clipboard. For all intents and purposes, graphics and frames act just like text when it comes to deleting them. To delete a graphic or a frame, simply select it and press the DEL key or CTRL-X. Any text surrounding the graphic or frame is reformatted after the element is removed from the document.

WHAT YOU NEED TO KNOW

Word for Windows allows you a great deal of control over where and how graphics are included in your document. In this lesson you have learned not just about graphics, but also about frames and how they can be used in your document. In particular, you have learned how to

- ☑ Insert a picture into text
- ☑ Insert a frame into text
- ☑ Insert a picture into a frame
- ☑ Adjust the size of a picture or frame
- ☑ Crop a picture or frame
- ☑ Adjust the size and position of a frame
- ☑ Wrap text around a frame
- ☑ Delete a graphic or frame

Lesson 34

Adding Drawings

In Lesson 33 you learned how you can add graphics to your document. That's great if you have graphics files that were created with a different program, but what if you just want to perform some simple drawings to enhance your document—for instance, you want to add a few lines or create a border?

Fortunately, Word for Windows includes a full-featured drawing package, which you can use to create such simple drawings. This software is included as a part of Word for Windows. In this lesson you will receive a quick introduction to how you use these features. You will learn

- How to display the Drawing toolbar
- What the tools allow you to do
- How to manipulate drawing objects

THE DRAWING TOOLBAR

The first step in creating a drawing is to display the Drawing toolbar. This is done by clicking on the 🖺 button on the Standard toolbar. When you click on this tool, Word for Windows switches to Page Layout viewing mode and displays the Drawing toolbar at the bottom of the document window:

Each of the tools on this toolbar allow you to create, modify, or manipulate drawing objects. These become a part of your Word for Windows document, but they can only be viewed in Page Layout viewing mode or in Print Preview. If you are familiar with other drawing programs, you will be comfortable with the tools on the Drawing toolbar with only a little practice. Table 34.1 describes the functions these tools perform:

Button	Function
	Draw lines
	Draw rectangles or squares
	Draw ellipses or circles
	Draw arcs
	Create a freeform drawing
	Create a text box
	Create a callout
	Format a callout
	Fill an object with a color
	Set a color for lines
	Set a line type
	Change back to a regular mouse pointer
	Bring object in front of other drawing objects
	Send object behind other drawing objects
	Bring object in front of any text
	Send object behind any text
	Group objects together
	Ungroup a previously grouped object
	Flip an object horizontally
	Flip an object vertically
	Rotate an object right by 90 degrees
	Reshape a free-form drawing object
	Control the drawing grid
	Align objects relative to each other
	Insert a picture container
	Insert a frame

Table 34.1 *Drawing toolbar button functions.*

DRAWING BASICS

As you can tell, the drawing toolbar within Word for Windows provides quite a few functions. Unfortunately, there are far to many to fully cover in this one lesson. However, the essence of the toolbar is experimentation, and you can try out any tool to see its effect within your document. There are a few tips, which will aid you in your drawings, however.

First, drawings are composed of *objects*. An object is an individual item, such as a line, an arc, an ellipse, or a rectangle. You can also create other types of objects such as text boxes and callouts. Each of these objects exists independently in the document, and can be moved at will.

As you position objects in relation to each other, you can create the appearance of other objects. For instance, you may draw two circles, one on top of each other, and then color them differently. This gives the appearance of a donut shape, although in reality it is two distinct objects. To facilitate the creation of compound objects, you can use the drawing toolbar to *group* or *ungroup* objects. Once grouped, using the ▣ tool, these objects can be moved about as if they were one object.

To arrange drawing objects relative to each other, you use the mouse and the two tools that allow you to adjust layer position. The ▣ tool allows you to move an object in front of other drawing objects, whereas the ▣ is used to move an object behind other objects.

You can perform the same function in relation to document text using the next two tools on the toolbar. For instance, you might want to move a circle behind a group of words. This is done using the ▣ tool, whereas the ▣ tool brings the drawing object in front of the text.

If you wish to delete a drawing object, simply select it and press the DEL key; it is removed from your drawing. You can also use the cut-and-paste functions of Word for Windows (described earlier in this book) to manipulate the objects.

Once you understand the concept of drawing objects and figure out their relationship to each other, you will find the Drawing toolbar extremely easy to use. In fact, you can create some stunning effects using these simple functions.

REMOVING THE DRAWING TOOLBAR

When you have finished with your drawing, you will want to remove the Drawing toolbar from the screen. This is done by again clicking on the ▣ tool on the Standard toolbar. This does not, however, return you to the viewing mode you were using before you displayed the toolbar. For instance, if you were using Normal viewing mode, you will not be returned to that mode. This is because your newly created drawings are only visible from Page Layout viewing mode, not from other viewing modes. If you manually change back to a different viewing mode, the drawings disappear from view. They are still there, as you will discover when you again change to Page Layout viewing mode, but they are simply not displayed.

WHAT YOU NEED TO KNOW

If you feel artistically inclined, Word for Windows includes a group of simple drawing tools you can use to add embellishments to your document. These functions, while not as powerful as those provided by many other commercial drawing programs, allow you to create and work with drawings easily. In this lesson you have learned:

- ☑ How to display the Drawing toolbar
- ☑ The functions you can perform with the drawing tools
- ☑ What drawing objects are and how they relate to each other
- ☑ How to delete and otherwise manipulate drawing objects
- ☑ How to remove the Drawing toolbar

In the next lesson you will round out your illustration skills by learning about Microsoft Graph.

Lesson 35

Using Microsoft Graph

Lesson 34 introduced you to the drawing tools provided with Word for Windows, which allow you to create drawings and include them in your documents. In this lesson you will learn about a program called Microsoft Graph. This software allows you to create graphs and charts, which you can add to your documents. You will learn how to

- Insert a chart

- Use Microsoft Graph

- Manipulate a graph or chart in your document

- Update your graph or chart

As you work though this lesson, remember that you are receiving a quick introduction. In reality, Microsoft Graph can be considered a miniature spreadsheet program. As such, its capabilities cannot be adequately covered in the course of one lesson. You should also remember that Microsoft Graph is not nearly as powerful as full-featured spreadsheet programs such as Excel. However, it is great for throwing together a few figures and creating a quick chart to illustrate a point in your document.

INSERTING A CHART INTO YOUR DOCUMENT

To create and insert a chart into your document, use the ▦ tool from the toolbar. When you click on this tool, Word for Windows assumes you want to insert a graph at the current cursor location. Your screen will appear as shown in Figure 35.1:

Menu

Datasheet

Chart

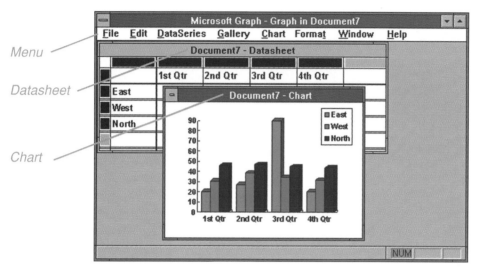

Figure 35.1 *The Microsoft Graph window.*

Notice that there are three major parts to the Microsoft Graph screen. If you are familiar with other spreadsheet programs (such as Excel), these parts might already seem familiar. The first part is the menu across the top of the window. This menu provides all the commands you can use to change how your data is presented. The second part is called the *datasheet.* This is analogous to a spreadsheet; it is where your raw data is contained. The final part is the *chart,* which is shown in the foreground. The chart is used to represent, in graphical format, the data contained in the datasheet.

Notice that when you first start Microsoft Graph, both the datasheet and the chart contain information. This is merely temporary information, which you can delete as necessary.

In the next few sections you will learn how you can enter data and create charts. When you have finished creating your chart, simply close the Microsoft Graph window. You will be asked if you want to update your document. If you click on Yes, the chart is inserted in your document. If you click on No, the chart is abandoned and, no changes are made to your document.

ENTERING DATA INTO A DATASHEET

To enter data into the datasheet, you must first select the datasheet. Click anywhere on the datasheet, and it will move to the foreground, in front of the chart. Then select the 16 cells (four rows deep and four columns wide) that make up the temporary data in the datasheet. If you press DEL, you can clear the contents of the cells. This gives you an empty datasheet, ready to receive your data.

Chances are pretty good that you have used a spreadsheet before. Entering data in a Microsoft Graph datasheet is virtually identical to entering information in a regular spreadsheet. The only difference is that you can only enter values—you cannot enter formulas. Enter your data, including any labels that you need for clarity or you want used in the chart. You might notice that as you input data, the information in the chart window is updated automatically.

There is one other feature with which you should be familiar. Notice that at the top of columns and to the left of rows in which you have data, there are black boxes. Other rows and columns don't have these; they have gray boxes. These boxes indicate that the data in the row or column is included in the chart. If you want to exclude rows or columns, all you need to do is select the row or column and then select Exclude Row/Col from the DataSeries menu. The chart will be updated immediately to reflect your action.

CHANGING THE TYPE OF CHART

If you select the chart window, you can modify how the chart appears. This is done by selecting a chart type from the Gallery menu shown in Figure 35.2:

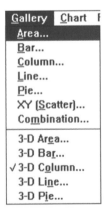

Figure 35.2 The Gallery menu.

When you select one of these 12 chart types, you are presented with pictures of charts you can select. For instance, if you select 3-D Bar from the Gallery menu, you are presented with five different types of 3-D bar charts, shown in Figure 35.3:

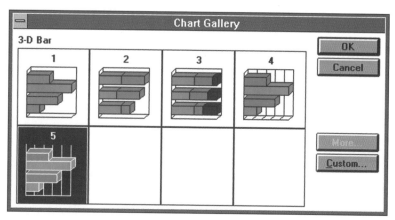

Figure 35.3 Choosing a 3-D bar chart.

To select a chart type, click on the chart and then on the OK button. The information in the datasheet is automatically reformatted into the selected chart type.

You can further refine how the chart appears by using the choices under the Chart and Format menus. Explaining each of the options under these menus would take more space than is available in this lesson, but you should feel free to experiment with each option to see what it does. Remember that you cannot hurt anything, and you don't have to use the chart in your document when you exit the program.

UPDATING A CHART

After you have inserted in your document a chart created with Microsoft Graph, you might want to update it. This is easily done because Word for Windows remembers the program you used to create the drawing. All you need to do is double-click on the chart, and the Microsoft Graph program is started automatically. However, instead of containing the temporary data, it will contain the data used to create the chart in your document. You can make any changes you desire and then update your document as you exit the program.

MOVING AND DELETING A CHART

In Lesson 34 you learned how you can move, size, and delete pictures. The same techniques are used to manipulate a chart created with Microsoft Graph. In fact, once you have placed the chart in your document, it is treated exactly the same as a picture. If you need a refresher, you might want to refer back to Lesson 34.

WHAT YOU NEED TO KNOW

If you are preparing a business report, it is not unusual to include charts and graphs to explain numerical data. Word for Windows makes this easy by providing you with a program to create charts. This program, Microsoft Graph, is easy to use—particularly for those who have used a spreadsheet before.

This lesson introduced you to the Microsoft Graph program; you learned

- ☑ How to start Microsoft Graph
- ☑ How to update your document with a chart created by Microsoft Graph
- ☑ The major parts of the Microsoft Graph window
- ☑ How to enter information in a datasheet
- ☑ How to select and modify a chart
- ☑ How to update a chart
- ☑ How to move and delete a chart

WORKING WITH TABLES

Section Seven

In Word for Windows, tables are treated differently than normal text. While it is possible to create tabular information (text in which each column is separated by tabs), identifying text as a table allows you much more freedom in formatting and placement of that information. With Word for Windows, you can easily control the column width and appearance of your tables, including adding borders and adjusting alignment.

Lesson 36

Adding a Table

Earlier in this book you learned that you can use tabs to create tabular information. For many purposes, tabs will work just fine. However, Word for Windows includes a table editor that allows you to work much easier with information in tabular format. This lesson introduces you to working with tables. Here you will learn:

- How to add a table to your document

- How to use the ▦ tool

- How to convert existing information to a table

- How to convert a table back to regular text

UNDERSTANDING TABLES

In Word for Windows, tables are self-contained units which you modify by using the Table menu. On the screen, an empty table generally looks like Figure 36.1:

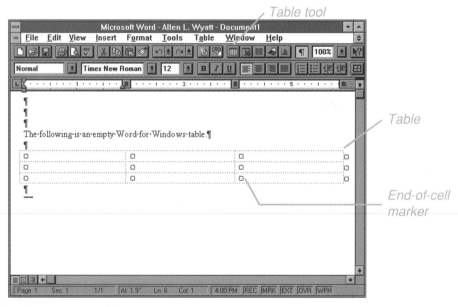

Figure 36.1 Inserting an empty table.

Notice the grid lines between rows and columns of the table. You determine how wide each column is, and the height of each row is determined automatically (after the table has been created you can format the height yourself if you wish). As the text within a *cell* (the intersection of a row and column) increases past the column width, it wraps to the next line and the cell is enlarged vertically to fit the text.

Notice, also, that there are end-of-cell markers located within each cell of the table. These markers are similar in nature to paragraph markers. As with paragraph markers, they contain the formatting information for the text in the cell. Since each cell in a table contains a marker like this, it means you can perform regular paragraph formatting on each cell within a table individually. Much of this formatting will be covered in the next two lessons.

ADDING A BLANK TABLE

To add a blank table to your document, position the cursor where you want the table to start. There are two ways you can then insert the table. The first is to use the 🗔 tool from the toolbar. When you click on this tool, you will see a small grid appear:

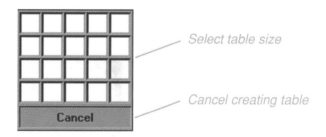

This grid allows you to set the size of table you want to use. Point to a cell, click and hold down the left mouse button, and drag the mouse until you have highlighted the number of rows and columns you want in the table. When you release the left mouse button, the table is inserted at the cursor.

Some readers might find it easier to create a table using the menus. This is done by choosing Insert Table from the Table menu. When you do, you will see the Insert Table dialog box shown in Figure 36.2:

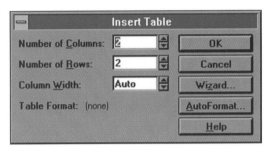

Figure 36.2 The Insert Table dialog box.

Here you can specify how many rows and columns you want in the table, as well as the width of each column. (You will learn more about column widths in the next lesson.) When you are satisfied with the dimensions of the table, click on the [OK] button. The table will appear at the current cursor position.

After you have inserted your table, you can add information to it as desired. You can position the cursor in any cell and begin typing. You can also insert graphics, charts, drawings, or other information within a cell. What you include is entirely up to you.

CONVERTING TEXT INFORMATION TO A TABLE

Since Word for Windows makes it so easy to work with tables using the table editor, you might want to convert your tabular material (tables created just with tab characters) into Word for Windows tables. This is easily done by using the Convert Text to Table option from the Table menu. However, to use this tool properly, you need to follow several steps:

1. Make sure there is only one tab between columns, no matter how funny it looks on the screen.

2. Select the paragraphs containing the tabular material.

3. Choose the Convert Text to Table option from the Table menu.

If you don't follow the first step, the table automatically created by Word for Windows will have too many columns in it, and you will have a bigger formatting job than you need. It is much easier to delete extra tabs before converting than it is to remove columns and reposition cells after converting.

CONVERTING A TABLE TO REGULAR TEXT

What if you want to convert a table to regular text? Word for Windows provides a way to do this automatically. The first step is to select the entire table. This is done by positioning the cursor in any cell of the table and then choosing Select Table from the Table menu.

Next, choose Convert Table to Text from the Table menu. In most cases Word for Windows will present you with a choice, as shown in Figure 36.3:

Figure 36.3 The Convert Table to Text dialog box.

Here you need to indicate if you want Word for Windows to use paragraph marks, tabs, commas, or custom characters (that you type into the field at the bottom of the window) to separate cells in the same row. Word for Windows always places a paragraph mark after the last cell in a row. For instance, let's assume you have a table like this:

one	two	three
four	five	six
seven	eight	nine
ten		twelve
	fourteen	fifteen

If you decide later to convert the table to text, using commas as the separator character, then the resulting text will look like this:

one, two, three
four, five, six
seven, eight, nine
ten, , twelve
, fourteen, fifteen

Notice that empty cells are still included in the converted text. They simply appear as lines with commas that separate no text.

WHAT YOU NEED TO KNOW

In this lesson you have started to learn about working with tables in Word for Windows. In particular, you have learned how:

- ☑ Word for Windows treats tables
- ☑ To add a table in Word for Windows
- ☑ To use the ⊞ tool
- ☑ To convert existing text to a table
- ☑ To convert tables back to text

In the next two lessons you will continue to learn more about how you can use tables effectively.

Lesson 37

Editing Your Table

In Lesson 36 you started to learn about tables. You learned how to add them to your document, as well as how to convert between regular text and a table. In this lesson you will learn more about working with tables. In particular, you will learn how to

- Change column width
- Select parts of a table
- Add rows and columns to your table
- Delete rows and columns from your table
- Move columns and rows
- Break one table into two tables

CHANGING COLUMN WIDTH

Hopefully you have already tried adding tables to your documents. If you have, you probably discovered that sometimes the automatic width feature used when adding tables doesn't always work well. It typically works well enough if you are adding a blank table, but doesn't work so well if you are converting existing text to a table. In these cases you will need to adjust the width of the columns in your table manually.

The easiest way to adjust column width is to use the ruler. To use the ruler to adjust column width, you must first move the cursor into the table. It doesn't matter where; any cell will do. Notice that the ruler changes to look like this:

Column dividers

The ruler is now divided into sections for each column in your table. The dividers between each section represent the column dividers. To adjust column width, point to one of these dividers with the mouse, click and hold down the left mouse button, and move the divider. When you release the mouse button, the table will be reformatted so the column divider is where you left it.

Another way to adjust the column width is to move the mouse cursor so it is positioned on the table grid line used to divide columns. You will know when the cursor is in the proper position because it will change to a movement tool with two arrowheads. Click and hold down the left mouse button. As you move the mouse, the divider grid is moved. When you release the mouse button, the column divider stays at that location.

Column adjustment cursor

Table grid lines

SELECTING PARTS OF A TABLE

As you learned in Lesson 36, there are times you need to select parts of a table. There are two general ways you can select parts of a table. The first is to use the menus; the other is to use the mouse.

The easiest selection operations to perform are to select individual cells and to select the entire table. You already learned how to select a table in Lesson 36. To select a cell, simply highlight the end-of-cell marker contained within each cell.

To select the row or column *in which the cursor is located*, choose the Select Row or Select Column options from the Table menu. To select a row with the mouse, however, move the mouse pointer to the left of the row and click the mouse button. To select a column, move the mouse cursor above the column (it will change to a downward-pointing arrow) and click the left mouse button.

ADDING AND REMOVING ROWS AND COLUMNS

Rows within a table do not always act like paragraphs. In fact, individual cells act more like paragraphs than rows do. For instance, you cannot position the cursor within the last cell of a row and press ENTER to add a new row. Instead, all you will do is add another line to the last cell in the row. Likewise, you cannot delete a row or column by selecting it and then pressing the DEL key. If you do, the text in each cell of the row or column will be cleared, but the row or column remains in the table.

There are three ways to add rows or columns to a table:

1. You can use the Insert Row or Insert Column options from the Table menu. When you choose the Insert Row option, a row is added above the currently selected row. When you use the Insert Column option, a column is added to the left of the selected column.

2. If you position the insertion point to the right of the last cell in a row (just before the end-of-row marker) and press ENTER, a new row will be inserted after the current row.

3. If you select a column and click the Table tool on the toolbar, a new column will be inserted. If your cursor is in a table with no selection and you click the Table tool, a new row will be inserted.

Note: *If you select all of the end-of-row markers in a table, you can add a column at the right side of a table. After selecting the markers, simply use any of the previously noted methods for adding a column.*

There are three ways to remove rows or columns:

1. You can select the rows or columns and use the Cut option from the Edit menu or press CTRL-X.

2. You can select the rows or columns and choose the Delete Row or Delete Column options from the Table menu.

3. If your cursor is in a table, but no selection is made, you can choose Delete Cells from the Table menu and then choose either Delete Entire Row or Delete Entire Column to delete the row or column your cursor is in.

The latter two methods will not store the row or column in the Clipboard, whereas the CTRL-X method will.

Moving Rows and Columns

If you already know how to move text using the Clipboard (as you learned in Lesson 8), you should have no problem moving rows and columns. The process is very similar. All you need to do is follow these steps:

1. Select the row or column you want to move.

2. Press CTRL-X. This cuts the row or column and retains it in the Clipboard.

3. Select the column to the right of where you want the column inserted, or select the row below where you want the row inserted.

4. Press CTRL-V. This inserts the row or column

Note: You can also click on the Cut and Paste tools on the toolbar, and you can also simply drag the selected row or column to a new spot in the table and drop it, just as you can drag and drop text.

BREAKING YOUR TABLE

There may be times when you need to break your table into two pieces. For instance, the table might run longer than a single page, and you need to insert some text at the top of the second page. This can't be done simply by pressing ENTER at the right place. Since Word for Windows treats tables differently than regular text, you must first *break* the table.

Breaking a table is done in one of two ways. Both ways require you to position the cursor in the row *after* where you want the break. After positioning the cursor, you can select Split Table option from the Table menu, or you can press CTRL-SHIFT-ENTER. Both result in adding a paragraph mark just before the current row.

WHAT YOU NEED TO KNOW

You have covered quite a bit in this lesson. Even though tables are treated differently than regular text, the basics of how they are treated are similar. This lesson covered the following:

- ☑ How to change column width
- ☑ How to select parts of a table
- ☑ Adding and deleting rows or columns
- ☑ Moving rows and columns
- ☑ Splitting your table in two

Once you learn the information in this lesson, you will be able to do practically anything with tables. If you doubt your ability to perform any of these functions, you might want to go back and review this lesson.

Lesson 38

Changing How Your Table Looks

In the last two lessons you have learned quite a bit about tables. There are still a few more details you should learn, however. In this lesson you will learn how you can change the looks of your table. Specifically, you will learn how to

- Turn off and on the grid lines

- Center a table on the page

- Add borders

CONTROLLING THE GRID

In Lesson 36 you learned that a table within Word for Windows appears as a grid made up of thin dotted lines. These gridlines do not appear on a printout; they only appear on the screen so you can easily locate and work with rows and columns in a table. Some people, however, might find this distracting.

If you want to, you can turn the gridlines off. To do this, choose the Gridlines option from the Table menu. This setting is a toggle—if a check mark appears beside option, then the gridlines appear on the screen. If there is no check mark, then the table appears without gridlines.

CENTERING A TABLE

In Lesson 37 you learned how you can adjust column widths in you table by using the ruler. You can also use the ruler to adjust where the table begins. This is done by moving the indent markers at the left side of the ruler, the same as you would move the column markers on the ruler.

Centering the table within the page margins is a little more convoluted, however. To do that, you should follow these steps:

1. Adjust the width of all your columns so you are satisfied with how your table looks.

2. Select the entire table.

3. Choose Cell Height & Width from the Table menu, and make sure the Row file card is selected. You will see the dialog box shown in Figure 38.1:

4. Make sure the value in the Indent from Left box is set to 0.

5. Choose Center from the Alignment box.

Row file card

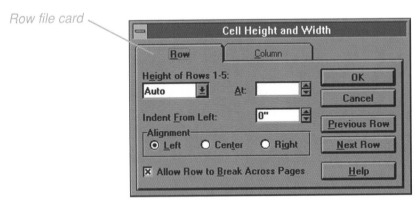

Figure 38.1 Cell Height and Width dialog box showing Row file card.

It might seem odd to you that the command to center a row, which is a horizontal alignment, is included under a menu option dealing with row height, which is a vertical formatting procedure. Don't feel like you are missing something—it is odd. No one has yet come up with a good reason why this capability is included under this menu choice.

ADDING BORDERS

In Lesson 32 you learned how to add borders to individual paragraphs in your document. You can also add printable borders to portions of your table, if you desire. This is done using the same Borders and Shading option from the Format menu. First you select the parts of the table that you want bordered and then you choose the menu option. You might want to refer back to Lesson 32 for a refresher on how to use the Borders and Shading dialog box.

Word for Windows also provides a simple way to add a printable grid to your entire table. Remember that the table gridlines you normally see on the screen are not printable; they only appear on the screen. To print a grid, you must select the entire table and then choose Borders and Shading from the Format menu. When you do, the Table Borders and Shading dialog box appears as shown in Figure 38.2:

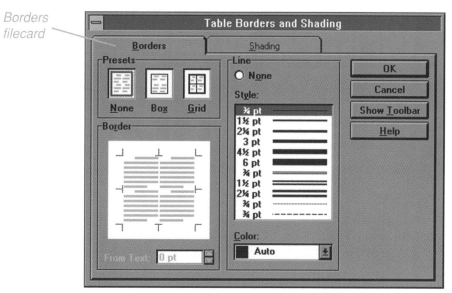

Borders filecard

Figure 38.2 Selecting a border for a table.

Notice that one of the presets in the upper-left corner of the dialog box is now called Grid. If you select this option, the grid is placed around each cell in your table.

WHAT YOU NEED TO KNOW

You now know virtually everything you need to know in order to work effectively with tables every day. Word for Windows includes a powerful table editor that allows you to treat tables as the special case they are. As you work with the table tools, you will come to appreciate them more and more.

This lesson has covered several formatting issues regarding tables. In particular, you should have learned how to do the following:

- ☑ Turn gridlines on and off
- ☑ Align and center the table between the text margins
- ☑ Add borders and a complete grid to your tables

Section Eight

WORD FOR WINDOWS SHORTCUTS

By this point you have learned how to use Word for Windows. Without learning anything else, you could use the program effectively and efficiently for all your word processing needs. There are shortcuts, however, which you can use to make your use of Word for Windows even more effective. This section will teach you how to use everything from AutoText to working with multiple documents and creating short macros. You will even learn how to change how Word for Windows starts, in order to begin using the program sooner. When you finish learning the information in this section, you will know as much as the experts—the only difference will be experience, which comes with time and use.

Lesson 39

Using AutoText

One of the features of Word for Windows that sets it apart from other word processors is referred to as *AutoText*. In previous versions of Word for Windows, AutoText used to be known as the *glossary*. It is a place where you can give names to blocks of text and later retrieve them using those names. This lesson will teach you how you can best use AutoText to improve your productivity. You will learn how to

- Create an AutoText entry

- Use an AutoText entry

- Delete an AutoText entry

- Print your AutoText entries

CREATING AN AUTOTEXT ENTRY

AutoText is stored within Word for Windows; and you can control the documents from which it is available. With AutoText, you can save a block of text and assign it a short name. You can later insert the block of text in your document by using the short name. You will learn how to do this in the next section.

The first step in using AutoText is to define an entry. For the sake of illustration, let's assume you work for the Acme Widget Company. If you prepare a lot of reports and documents for your company, you might get tired of typing out the company name all the time. This is where the glossaries come in handy.

To assign the name to an AutoText entry, select the company name. Whatever text you include in the selection will be included in the AutoText entry. Make sure you don't include the space after the company name in the selection. Next, choose the AutoText option from the Edit menu, or click on the 🔳 button on the Standard toolbar. Either way, you will see the AutoText dialog box, similar to Figure 39.1:

Short name

Selected text

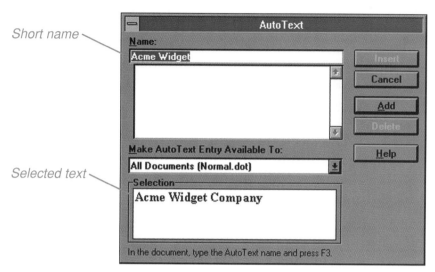

Figure 39.1 The AutoText dialog box.

In the Name box, enter the name you want to use for the AutoText entry (Word for Windows suggests a possible name for you to use). You can use any name you desire, including names that have spaces in them. It is generally a good idea to use a short name, yet one that is long enough that you don't easily forget what it means. In our example case, you may want to use the name **AWC**. Upper or lowercase letters don't matter; you can enter them any way you desire.

Once the name has been entered, click on the ⬚ Add ⬚ button. This saves the selected text as an AutoText entry using the name you provided. In our example, the name Acme Widget Company is assigned to the name AWC.

If you choose an AutoText entry name that is already defined, then you are asked to confirm that you want to overwrite the current definition. Click on the ⬚ Yes ⬚ button to do so.

Note: You can assign virtually anything that you desire to an AutoText entry. For instance, you can assign a letterhead salutation that takes several lines, or you can assign a graphic, picture, or chart. What you assign to an AutoText entry is entirely up to you.

USING AUTOTEXT

Once you have defined an AutoText entry, you can use it anywhere you want. This is done in one of several ways. The easiest way is to simply type the AutoText entry name (such as *AWC*) and then press the **F3** key or click on the 🖺 tool. Word for Windows immediately searches for an AutoText entry with the same name as the preceding word or phrase. If a match is found, the AutoText name is removed from the document and replaced with the full text of the AutoText entry. Thus, you could type **AWC**, immediately press the **F3** key, and the characters A-W-C would be replaced with *Acme Widget Company.* Using AutoText in this way saves, in this example, 15 keystrokes—you can use four keystrokes to type what otherwise would have required 19.

The other ways to use an AutoText entry involve using the menus. Using these methods, you do not have to type the AutoText name. Instead, you choose the AutoText option from the Edit menu, after which you will see the AutoText dialog box, as shown in Figure 39.2:

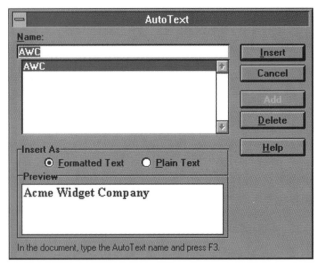

Figure 39.2 The AutoText dialog box.

Using the mouse, select the AutoText entry you want to use. Under the AutoText name list, indicate whether you want the entry inserted as Formatted Text or Plain Text. Click on the [Insert] button, and the text is inserted. While both choices result in the AutoText being entered in your document at the cursor location, one of them strips the characters of any formatting they may have. How you insert the AutoText entry is up to you.

DELETING AN AUTOTEXT ENTRY

If you use AutoText quite a bit, you will find that your entries tend to be rather short-lived and dynamic. For instance, you might create an AutoText entry or two for a specific project. After the project, you no longer need the AutoText entries. Over time, your AutoText list might become quite cluttered with older entries that you no longer need.

To review and delete AutoText entries, you again choose the AutoText option from the Edit menu. You will see the AutoText dialog box, and you can select individual AutoText entries from the list provided. As you select them, their name appears in the AutoText Name box, and a number of the characters in the AutoText entry appear at the bottom of the dialog box. If you decide that you no longer need the entry, simply click on the ▭ Delete ▭ button. The entry is immediately removed.

PRINTING YOUR AUTOTEXT ENTRIES

Word for Windows also allows you to print a copy of your AutoText entries. This is helpful if you have lots of entries you might want to delete, or if you simply want a record of how you have defined your AutoText. To print the AutoText entries, choose the Print option from the File menu. You will see the Print dialog box as shown in Figure 39.3:

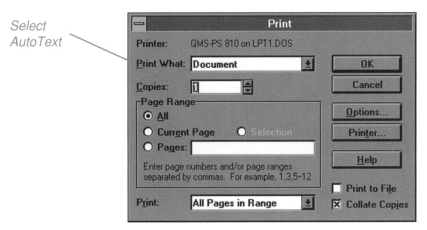

Figure 39.3 The Print dialog box.

In the Print What field, choose AutoText Entries. When you click on the ▭ OK ▭ button, the AutoText entries will be printed.

WHAT YOU NEED TO KNOW

AutoText is one of the biggest time savers in Word for Windows. It allows you to assign blocks of text to a short name, which you can later use to recall the block of text. This capability helps increase productivity and speed. You should now know to do the following:

- ☑ Define an AutoText entry
- ☑ Reuse an AutoText entry by using the name again
- ☑ Expand an AutoText entry in your document
- ☑ Delete an AutoText entry
- ☑ Print your AutoText entries

Lesson 40

Working with Different Parts of the Same Document

As you begin to work with longer and longer documents, you will find that there are times you need to refer to information located on different pages of your document. For instance, you might be developing some detail information based on a numbered list that occurred earlier in your document. If the numbered list appeared on page 2 and the detail information is being written on page 5, it can be bothersome to flip back and forth between the pages.

Fortunately, Word for Windows provides a quick and simple way to look at different parts of the same document. In this lesson you will learn:

- What document panes are

- How to open a pane

- How you can control the size of document panes

- How you can switch between panes

- How to close a pane

WHAT ARE PANES?

A *document pane* is simply a different view of the same document. Word for Windows allows you to open a document pane so you can view two different parts of the same document. You can open a document pane by using the *document pane bar*. This is a small, thick bar located at the top of the vertical scroll bar on the right side of your document window as shown here:

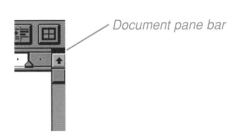

Document pane bar

When you move the mouse cursor over the top of this bar, it changes to indicate you can grab the bar. If you click and hold down the left mouse button, you can drag the pane bar downward. When you release the mouse button, the document window is split in two, as shown in Figure 40.1:

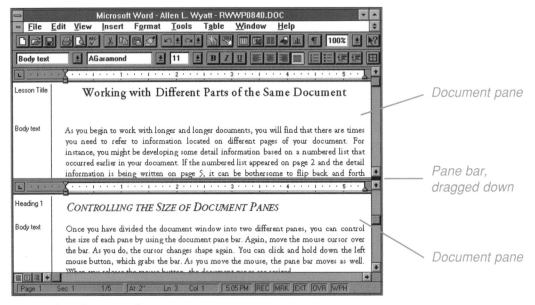

Figure 40.1 Dragging down a new pane.

If you double-click on the document pane bar Word for Windows will divide the document window in half automatically.

Note: You can also split a document window into panes by using the Split option from the Window menu. Using this option allows you to adjust the position of the divider using the mouse. When you click on the left mouse button or press Enter, the window is split at that position.

CONTROLLING THE SIZE OF DOCUMENT PANES

Once you have divided the document window into two different panes, you can control the size of each pane by using the document pane bar. Again, move the mouse cursor over the bar. As you do, the cursor changes shape again. You can click and hold down the left mouse button, which grabs the bar. As you move the mouse, the pane bar moves as well. When you release the mouse button, the document panes are resized.

JUMPING BETWEEN PANES

Each pane in a document window is independent of the other. You can move from one pane to the other by simply using the mouse. Point into one pane and click the mouse button, and that pane becomes active. The cursor appears, and any text you type will appear at the cursor location in that pane.

If you want to move to the other pane, use the mouse cursor to point to the other pane. When you click the mouse button, that pane becomes active. If you would rather not keep grabbing the mouse to switch between panes, you can use the **F6** key. Pressing the key will switch between the panes on the screen.

Notice that the text in each pane can be scrolled up and down independently. Each pane has its own vertical scroll bar. This means, as in the example provided at the first of this lesson, you could view page 2 of your document in one pane and page 5 in the other.

Even though vertical scrolling is independent, horizontal scrolling is not. There is still only one horizontal scroll bar, located at the bottom of the document widow. Also, you should realize that panes only allow you to see two different places of the same document. If you make changes in one pane, they are automatically made in the other, since it represents the same document.

CLOSING A DOCUMENT PANE

One of the drawbacks to working with document panes is that you cannot see as much of the document as you could if you weren't using panes. Thus, you will probably want to close the second document pane when you have finished whatever you need it for.

To close a document pane, simply double-click on the document pane bar. When you do, it moves to the top of the vertical scroll bar, thereby removing the second document pane. You can also use the Remove Split option from the Window menu.

Note: You can also close a pane by using the mouse to drag the document pane bar to the top or bottom of the window.

WHAT YOU NEED TO KNOW

Document panes can be used to view different parts of the document on which you are working. If you find yourself jumping back and forth between two locations in a document quite a bit, you should divide the document window into panes so you can work on both parts of the document at once.

In this lesson you should have learned the following:

☑   Word for Windows allows you to divide a document window into panes.

☑   Document panes allow you to view two different parts of the same document.

☑   You can scroll the document panes up and down independently.

☑   How to change the size of the document panes.

☑   How to jump between panes.

☑   How to close a document pane.

Lesson 41

Working with More Than One Document

In Lesson 40 you learned how you can divide your document window into individual panes, which allow you to view different parts of the same document. But what if you want to work with multiple documents, not with just one? Word for Windows also allows you to do this quickly and easily. In this lesson you will learn how to

- Open multiple documents

- Jump between different document windows

- View more than one document window at a time

- Save all your open documents

OPENING MULTIPLE DOCUMENTS

In Lesson 11 you learned how to load a document. Since that time, you have been working with only one document at a time. However, Word for Windows will allow you to open more than one document at a time. Each document has its own document window, which you can switch between.

For instance, let's assume you are working on a report for your business. This is a monthly report, and you want to compare last month's report to the one you are working on for this month. Since Word for Windows allows you to have more than one document open at a time, you can have both this month's report and last month's report open at the same time. Later in this lesson you will learn how you can even view both files at once.

To open multiple documents, just open them as you would your original document. You can use any of the techniques described in Lesson 11. There is another way to open multiple documents, however. Word for Windows will allow you to open multiple copies of the same document. This is done either by loading the same document again, or by choosing the New Window option from the Window menu. If you do this, notice that Word for Windows changes the filename which appears in the title bar. It appends a colon and a window number after the filename, as shown in the following:

Indicates second window

Microsoft Word - RBWFW35.DOC:2

In this instance, Word for Windows has appended a colon and a 2, indicating this is the second window for this file. You can work in either window you want; the changes you make in one are automatically reflected in the other.

JUMPING BETWEEN DOCUMENT WINDOWS

To change from one window to the other, use the Window menu. When you pull down this menu, you will see a list of document windows available:

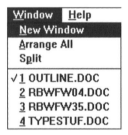

The currently active document window is marked with a check mark. You can select a different window by clicking on the document name with the mouse. You can also switch between document windows by pressing ALT-F6 or CTRL-F6. These key combinations will cycle you forward through the document windows. You can cycle backward by pressing SHIFT-ALT-F6 or SHIFT-CTRL-F6. If you have several document windows open, you will probably find it easier to use the menu than to cycle through the windows using the keyboard.

VIEWING MORE THAN ONE DOCUMENT AT A TIME

In addition to allowing you to open multiple documents, Word for Windows also allows you to adjust the size of the document windows. This is done in much the same way as when you use individual windows in the Windows operating system. In Word for Windows, as in Windows, you can adjust window sizes so you can see more than one document window at a time.

The quickest way to do this is to select the Arrange All option from the Window menu. Doing this will divide the Word for Windows program window into as many pieces as necessary to display all of the open documents. Thus, if you have two documents loaded, your screen is divided in half. Three documents results in each one occupying a third of your screen.

If you have lots of documents loaded, then you might find that the Arrange All option results in your screen looking cluttered. However, it is still a good place to start. You can then adjust the size of individual document windows using the window sizing techniques described in Lesson 3.

SAVING ALL YOUR DOCUMENTS

As you come to rely more and more upon Word for Windows, it is not unusual to have two, three, or more documents open at the same time. As you switch between document windows and make changes in the files, you will want to save your changes. It can be very time consuming to switch between the windows and click on the 🖫 tool. If you had three open documents, that would mean three switches and three uses of the tool.

Instead, Word for Windows provides a way you can save changes to all of the documents (and any template files which might have changed) with one command. To do this, select the Save All option from the File menu. Word for Windows then updates all open files and saves your changes to disk.

WHAT YOU NEED TO KNOW

Word for Windows is a powerful word processor that allows you to work on multiple documents simultaneously. This is done by simply opening the documents on which you want to work. In this lesson you have learned the following skills:

- ☑ How to open more than one document
- ☑ How to switch between document windows
- ☑ How to adjust document window size
- ☑ How to save all of your open files

Lesson 42

Creating Short Macros

Word for Windows includes a full-featured *macro command language*, which allows you to create your own commands. This macro language is called WordBasic, and is based on the BASIC programming language. This gives it an enormous amount of power and flexibility.

This lesson will not cover everything there is to know about Word for Windows' macro language. That amount of detail would take far more space than is available in this whole book. In this lesson you will learn the following, however:

- How to record short macros
- Where macros are stored
- How to run a macro
- What else you can do with macros
- Where you can get more information

HOW TO RECORD A MACRO

A *macro* is a command or series of commands you can write or a series of movements you can record that is activated by one command. There are two ways you can create Word for Windows macros. The first is to record them using the macro recorder. The other way is to write them from scratch using the macro editor. The latter method of writing macros is beyond the scope of this book, so the discussion here will focus on the first method.

Anything you do in Word for Windows that is of a repetitive nature is a good candidate for a macro. For instance, if you find yourself repeatedly formatting a paragraph a certain way, then you can consolidate several steps into a single macro. As an example, you could create a macro to do the following:

1. Jump to the beginning of the current paragraph
2. Format the paragraph using a defined style

3. Highlight the first word

4. Format the word as bold

5. Add a period after the word, followed by two spaces

6. Jump to the beginning of the next paragraph

7. Save the document

If you had to do these seven steps manually over numerous repetitions, you could expend a lot to time and energy. If you were to record these steps in a macro, however, you could just let Word for Windows do the work—all you would do is issue one command.

To record a macro, choose the Macro option from the Tools menu. When the Macro dialog box is displayed, click on the ⬚ Record... button. You will then see the Record Macro dialog box shown in Figure 42.1:

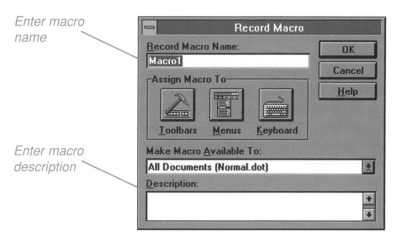

Figure 42.1 The Record Macro dialog box.

Here you can specify four things. In the Record Macro Name field, you should provide a name you want used for this macro. You can accept the default name, if you desire, but if you plan on using the macro more than once, you will want to use a more descriptive name.

In the Description box, at the bottom on the dialog box, you can optionally provide a comment about your macro. This might come in helpful if you later want to remember what the macro is for.

In the Make Macro Available To field, you can specify where you want the macro available. Click on the arrow to the right of the field, and then select whether it should be available globally or just to documents using the template. Where you store it is up to you and what you plan on doing with the macro.

In the middle of the dialog box is an area where you can indicate whether you want the macro assigned to a toolbar, a menu, or the keyboard. You don't have to assign it to one of these, but you can if you desire. For instance, you could assign the macro to the key combination SHIFT-CTRL-T or some other combination that you desire.

If you choose to assign the macro to a toolbar, a menu, or the keyboard, you will see the appropriate dialog box that allows you to make the assignment. After you have done so, you can click on the [OK] button; it is the same as clicking on [OK] from the Record Macro dialog box.

Once you click on the [OK] button, Word for Windows displays the macro recorder buttons, alters the mouse cursor, and starts recording everything you do. The macro recorder buttons and altered mouse cursor look like this:

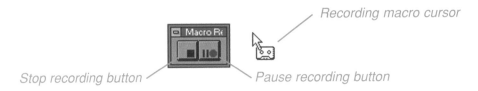

Recording macro cursor

Stop recording button   *Pause recording button*

You should then start going through the steps you want the macro to perform. In the example provided earlier, you would start manually doing the seven steps. When you have finished with the steps you want in the macro, choose the Stop button (the left one) from the macro recorder buttons. The macro is then saved and available for use at any time.

How to Run a Macro

There are two ways you can run a macro. If you defined a keypress, menu option, or toolbar tool you could use to start the macro, then one of those options is the quickest way to invoke it. For instance, if you assigned your macro to SHIFT-CTRL-T, then pressing those keys will start executing the steps you recorded in the macro.

The other way to run a macro is to select the Macro option from the Tools menu. When you do, you will see the Macro dialog box, similar to the one shown in Figure 42.2:

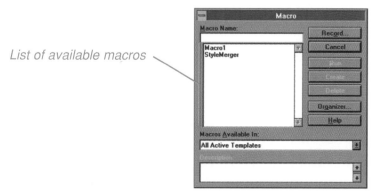

List of available macros

Figure 42.2 The Macro dialog box.

The defined macros are shown in the list at the left of the dialog box. You can select a macro from those in the list and then click on the [Run] button. The macro is executed immediately.

OTHER MACRO CAPABILITIES

Macros can be used to do just about anything you want. The only real limit is your imagination and your knowledge of how to use the macro language. After you record your first macros, you can later edit them using the macro editor. (You probably noticed the [Edit] button on the Macro dialog box shown in the last section.) Editing macros takes additional information about what the WordBasic commands and keywords are, however.

Once you have defined your macros, you can then do other things with them, such as assigning the macro to a toolbar tool or adding a menu option that runs the macro. In fact, you can use macros to completely customize the menu structure and toolbar used in Word for Windows.

WHERE YOU CAN GET MORE INFORMATION

There have been entire books written on the topic of developing Word for Windows macros. If you want more information on this topic, you should refer to any of the following:

- The WordBasic online help (from the Help menu)
- *1001 Word for Windows Tips,* written by Allen L. Wyatt and published by Jamsa Press
- *Hacker's Guide to Word for Windows,* written by Woody Leonhard and Vincent Chen, and published by Addison-Wesley

WHAT YOU NEED TO KNOW

This lesson has provided you with a very brief introduction to Word for Windows macros. You have learned

- ☑ What a macro is
- ☑ How to record a macro
- ☑ How to run a macro
- ☑ What you can do with macros
- ☑ Where to get more information

Perhaps the best way to learn more about macros is just to begin using them. Identify some simple tasks that you want to use macros for and then record them. As you work with them more and more, you will become more confident, and you can customize Word for Windows to truly reflect the way you work.

Lesson 43

Changing How Word for Windows Starts

At the very beginning of this book you learned how to start Word for Windows. In Lesson 1 you learned that you start Word for Windows by double-clicking on the Word for Windows icon in the Program Manager. While this is the most direct way to begin the program, there are other ways you can change how Word for Windows starts. In this lesson you will learn a few of those ways, including how to

- Start Word for Windows with no document

- Start Word for Windows with a specific document

- Start Word for Windows whenever you start Windows

- Execute a macro automatically when you start Word for Windows

STARTING WITH NO DOCUMENT

Normally, when you start Word for Windows, it starts with a fresh document window open, ready for you to start typing. To many people this is a waste of time, because they normally begin working on existing documents instead of starting a new one—they just have to close the new window.

You can configure Word for Windows to start with no document. This is done not from within Word for Windows, but from the Program Manager. The first step is to select the Word for Windows program icon by clicking on it with the mouse. Don't double-click on it; that will start the program. Simply highlight the Word for Windows icon.

Next, using the Program Manager menus, choose Properties from the File menu. You will see the Program Item Properties dialog box, which should look like Figure 43.1:

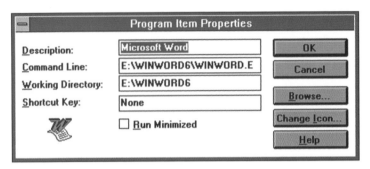

Figure 43.1 Program Item Properties dialog box.

Notice the second field is labeled Command Line. This is the actual operating system command necessary to run Word for Windows. Select this field and move the cursor to the very right side of the command line. The command line should end with the Word for Windows program name, which is WINWORD.EXE. Change the command line so it looks like this:

E:\WINWORD6\WINWORD.EXE /N

The DOS path provided to the left of WINWORD.EXE might be different on your system. That's OK; it just means that your Word for Windows program is stored in a different place than mine. The important change here is to add the /N after the program name. This instructs Word for Windows to start with no document.

Once you have finished making the changes to the Command Line field, click on the [OK] button. When you later start Word for Windows, there will be no empty document waiting for you to start typing. Instead, you will need to open a document file explicitly.

STARTING WITH A SPECIFIC DOCUMENT

You can also instruct Word for Windows to start with a particular document already loaded. This process is similar to the one described in the last section. Instead of adding /N to the command line, you will add a filename. For instance, if you wanted Word for Windows to always start with a file called OUTLINE.DOC loaded, your command line would be

E:\WINWORD6\WINWORD.EXE OUTLINE.DOC

You can use any other filename you desire, however you should remember to use a full pathname if the file is not located in the same directory as Word for Windows.

STARTING WORD FOR WINDOWS WHEN YOU START WINDOWS

If you use Word for Windows a lot, you will probably want to always have it available to use. This is most easily done by starting Word for Windows whenever you start Windows. To do this, you simply need to have the Word for Windows icon in the Startup program group. This can be done by moving the Word for Windows program icon to the Startup group, but this might not be a good idea. Most people who configure Windows to automatically start Word for Windows move only a *copy* of the Word for Windows icon to the Startup program group. In this way they will always know that they can also start Word for Windows from their Word for Windows program group, if necessary.

To create a copy of the Word for Windows icon, open the Word for Windows program group. Select the Word for Windows program icon by clicking on it with the mouse. Don't double-click on it; that will start the program. Simply highlight the Word for Windows icon.

Next, choose the Copy option from the File menu in the Program Manager. You will see the Copy Program Item dialog box shown in Figure 43.2:

Select Startup group

Figure 43.2 Program Item Properties dialog box.

In the To Group field, specify the Startup group. When you click on [OK], the program item (the Word for Windows program icon) is copied to the Startup group.

Note: You can also copy the Word for Windows icon to the Startup group by CTRL-dragging with the mouse. With both the Word for Windows icon and the Startup group visible on the screen, hold down the CTRL key, click on the Word for Windows icon, and drag a copy of the icon over into the Startup group. Release the mouse button, and the icon will be copied into the group.

Now open the Startup group and select the Word for Windows program icon there. Again, don't double-click on it; that will start the program. Simply highlight the icon. Now choose Properties from the File menu in the Program Manager. You will see the Program Item Properties dialog box, which should look similar to that shown in Figure 43.3:

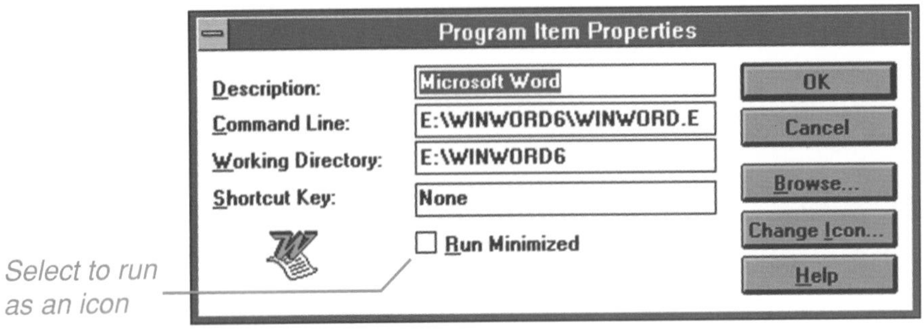

Figure 43.3 Program Item Properties dialog box.

Make sure the check box labeled Run Minimized is selected, and then click on the [OK] button. This ensures that when Word for Windows starts, it will be automatically minimized as an icon at the bottom of the Windows desktop.

RUNNING A MACRO AUTOMATICALLY

In Lesson 42 you learned how to record macros. If you want, you can create a macro that runs whenever you start Word for Windows. For instance, you might want several documents loaded automatically, and the program window maximized. Since this process involves multiple steps, it is an ideal candidate for a macro. To have a macro run automatically whenever you start Word for Windows, all you need to do is use the macro name AutoExec. Make sure it is saved as a global macro, and it will run every time you start the program.

WHAT YOU NEED TO KNOW

There are many ways you can start Word for Windows. In this lesson you have learned of some changes you can make that will affect how you start your session with Word for Windows. You have learned how to

- ☑ Start Word for Windows with no document
- ☑ Start Word for Windows with a specific document
- ☑ Start Word for Windows automatically when Windows starts
- ☑ Run a macro automatically when Word for Windows starts

By combining the starting methods in this lesson, you can get to work quicker and more easily.

Index